Literacy Experiences of Formerly Incarcerated Women

Literacy Experiences of Formerly Incarcerated Women

Sentences and Sponsors

Melanie N. Burdick

LEXINGTON BOOKS
Lanham • Boulder • New York • London

Published by Lexington Books
An imprint of The Rowman & Littlefield Publishing Group, Inc.
4501 Forbes Boulevard, Suite 200, Lanham, Maryland 20706
www.rowman.com

6 Tinworth Street, London SE11 5AL, United Kingdom

British Library Cataloguing in Publication Information Available

Library of Congress Cataloging-in-Publication Data

Names: Burdick, Melanie N., 1970– author.
Title: Literacy experiences of formerly incarcerated women : sentences and sponsors / Melanie N. Burdick.
Description: Lanham, Maryland : Lexington Books, an imprint of The Rowman & Littlefield Publishing Group, Inc., [2021] | Includes bibliographical references and index. | Summary: "This book depicts results from narrative research involving four formerly incarcerated women and how they used literacy experiences to reconfigure their identities, overcome stigma, and gain control over their lives. The author discusses issues including literacy and motherhood, prison libraries, and transitions from prison to college classrooms."—Provided by publisher.
Identifiers: LCCN 2021006381 (print) | LCCN 2021006382 (ebook) | ISBN 9781793615237 (cloth) | ISBN 9781793615244 (epub) | ISBN 9781793615251 (pbk)
Subjects: LCSH: Women ex-convicts—Books and reading. | Women ex-convicts—Social conditions. | Literacy.
Classification: LCC HV9275 .B87 2021 (print) | LCC HV9275 (ebook) | DDC 302.2/244086927—dc23
LC record available at https://lccn.loc.gov/2021006381
LC ebook record available at https://lccn.loc.gov/2021006382

Contents

Acknowledgments

First and foremost, I want to thank the four women who are the beating hearts behind this book. Diane, Lexi, Grace, and Becky generously shared their time and stories with me. The time I spent with each woman changed the way I see my roles as a professor, parent, and citizen. I have endeavored to represent their words authentically and honestly, and I hope that I have come close to presenting them as they would like the world to see them. It was a true honor to be entrusted with their stories. I also want to thank my formerly incarcerated students past and present, who have inspired me to become a better teacher. I must thank the women I have taught at the Topeka Correctional Facility in the Sisters of Survival writing group for all they have shown me about storytelling, writing, and learning.

Many, many thanks go to my wise and dedicated colleagues who teach in the Criminal Justice and Legal Studies Department at Washburn University: Dr. Patricia Dahl, Dr. Melanie Worsley, and Dr. Erin Grant. Each of these women ignored our academic silos and generously advised me in this research project. They provided feedback on early drafts, pointed me toward important scholarship in the field of criminal justice, and patiently answered what probably seemed like a lot of basic or even silly questions. These scholars filled many holes in my knowledge of the criminal justice system and never made me feel inferior when I asked for their help.

Thank you to Dr. Vanessa Steinroetter, Dr. Laura Stephenson, and Dr. JuliAnn Mazachek who approved of and supported me in my academic sabbatical. This provided me with the most valuable gift—of time—enabling me to focus on writing this manuscript. Huge thanks to Catlynn Jaynes, Sue Taylor-Owens, and Dr. Jericho Hockett, who adjusted their workloads for a semester to cover my administrative duties during this sabbatical. Many thanks to other colleagues of mine at Washburn who provided friendship and kindly showed interest and support in countless ways: Eric McHenry, Dennis Etzel, Jr., Liz Derrington, Izzy Wasserstein, Karen Barron, Dr. David Weed, Dr. Tracy Routsong, and Dr. Kelly Erby.

Members of the Greater Kansas City Writing Project also assisted me with early drafts of certain chapters. Thank you to Ted Fabiano, Jeff Dierking, Mary Engler, Leayn Losh, Kate Kraybill, and Paige Mulvihill for providing me with astute feedback and encouragement. Other writing friends, Dr. Jane Greer, Elizabeth Schurman, Dr. Laura Murphy, Dr. Muffy Walter, and Dr. Louise Krug, accompanied me on writing retreats and writing dates and listened as I talked through ideas connected to this book. Their companionship and support ensured the work got done and that I felt less isolated doing it.

Finally, much gratitude goes to my husband, Bob, and my sons, Charlie, Simon, George, and Pete. You all have supported me beyond expectations. You keep my heart buoyant and my eyes clear. I am so thankful to have you in my life.

Preface

In her article, "Poor Teeth," author Sarah Smarsh describes how rising out of her family's poverty would forever influence her interactions with the world around her: "but in my academic and professional 'climbing,' I learnt early and often that one doesn't leave a place, class or culture and enter another, but rather holds the privilege and burden of many narratives simultaneously" (2017). Like Smarsh, we all live through multiple narratives, and in listening to another's experiences, we story them by weaving through our personal stories already made manifest. This preface serves the purpose of identifying, like Smarsh, "the privilege and burden of many narratives" that I carry as a researcher and how they have provided lenses through which I have engaged in this research and writing about the literacy experiences of formerly incarcerated women.

This book is theoretically and methodologically based in narrative inquiry (Clandinin and Connelly 2000). The goals of narrative researchers are not to merely record and present stories, but to inquire into the how and the why certain stories are told. Also important is how the tellings uncover, conceal, provide advantages, or constrain lives of storytellers. While describing the framework for narrative inquiry Clandinin and Connelly wrote: "we are not merely objective inquirers, people on the high road, who study a world lesser in quality than our moral temperament would have it, people who study a world we did not help create. On the contrary, we are complicit in the world we study . . . we work in the space not only with our participants but also with ourselves" (2000).

As a researcher, I must then confront what I bring to the stories I hear, construct, and analyze. I must reflect upon and confront the reasons I come to this research and how I reinforce or challenge certain stories. Feminist theory, which also informs my work, identifies both dangers and responsibilities in speaking on behalf of others. Researchers must be fully transparent in the ways they are possibly constrained or liberated by certain narratives and the ways they may inadvertently constrain or liberate narrators that they represent. For these reasons, I will preface this research with an explanation into my own context and point of view, and I will share my stories of why I have come to this research.

RESEARCHERS, STORIES, AND FEMINIST UNDERSTANDINGS

In all qualitative research, the researcher must be clear and conscious of her positioning toward the topic, the research questions, and the participants. This is important because when we try to uncover the lived experience of participants, the researchers' lived experiences will always color and influence the data collection and findings (Clandinin and Connelly 2000; Cresswell 2006; Denzin and Lincoln 2005; Lincoln and Guba 1985; Polkinghorne 1988). This can come through unintended and unconscious biases, but it can also come through faulty assumptions, or the projection of the researchers experiences upon those of the participants. With narrative research, it is even more important that a researcher identify and clearly acknowledge her biases in order to identify where her story ends and the participants' stories begin. While we all live life through the storying of our experiences, a researcher must clearly delineate who is storying the data and how a participants' storying may fit into her own personal narratives as well as her understanding of scholarship and even larger social narratives.

When we look at feminist theories of communication and research, there is a clear declaration against assumptions of traditional research: that it is linear, the researcher is assumed to be detached and unbiased; the data collection and analysis is fact-driven; the results are replicable. Traditional research reproduces masculine ways of understanding and as such has historically ignored or flattened the lived experiences of women and other underrepresented groups. As I bring feminist theories into my own research and writing, I must continue to answer and echo these declarations, and I do so by making myself visible as a researcher. I do so by acknowledging that it is my own experience through which I have come to understand the initial problem that initiated my research; the data, its collection and analysis; and the resulting information from my research process.

I am writing this preface from a more personal stance than what many expect from a research monograph. The tone will be more informal than the rest of the book, and I am clearly positioning my own voice within this study. While the rest of this book will be focused upon the participants, their stories, and their lived experiences, this introduction will tell my stories and to the best of my ability, uncover for my readers how I came to this work, why, and how my storying of my past, present, and future have intertwined with the stories of my participants.

MY STORIES OF TEACHING AND LEARNING

My academic specialty is in the teaching of writing, and I have spent over twenty years teaching others how to write while researching ways to do this better. Writing is often a politically fraught act. At the same time, I see literacy in general and writing in particular as an assortment of seemingly magical acts where a person can better learn about oneself, understand and define one's identity, clarify one's past and set goals for the future. Through reading a variety of perspectives, one is more apt to empathize and interact with diverse groups (Nussbaum 1998). The act of writing persuasively to a variety of audiences within varied contexts ensures a wealth of social capital (Brandt 1998; Freire and Macedo 1987; Gee 2015; New London Group 1996). I regularly teach introductory and advanced college composition classes, and while many outside the field of writing studies might believe that the teaching of writing focuses mainly around issues of grammar, mechanics, and word choice, these are but tiny pieces of the actual curriculum. When I teach writing, I create opportunities for students to examine rhetorical contexts, the power structures that complicate and define these contexts, and the ways in which they can effectively negotiate messages given and received. As I worked through my research process, I observed my participants narratives of literacy experiences as narratives of power seized, withheld, discovered, or denied.

Lately much of my professional work has focused upon inclusivity in pedagogy and ways I and other faculty can create spaces that are welcoming and accessible to all students. Higher education is a transformative experience that for many can feel unwelcoming or inaccessible, and I have made it a priority in my work to find ways to destroy barriers that may stand in the way for some of our most underserved or oppressed citizens to get a college education. This study is certainly affected by my thinking and work in this area as I believe that formerly incarcerated individuals (especially women) are some of our most vulnerable citizens and can greatly benefit from the transformational possibilities of becoming more literate and more educated.

While the previous discussion covers my expertise and current interests in the teaching of writing and inclusive pedagogy, it is just as important that I share where I may lack extensive training. My degrees and research have been firmly situated within the field of rhetoric and composition, and the scholarship of teaching and learning; I do not have formal training in the fields of criminology or criminal justice. I have endeavored to educate myself regarding the field of criminal justice through extensive reading and numerous conversations with colleagues and friends in my university's criminal justice and legal studies department. I have also learned from my own experience teaching creative writing classes within a medium/maximum security women's prison. However, I must acknowledge that the analysis and commentary regarding the data within this book will be filtered through a lens that is less positioned within the field of criminal justice and more firmly rooted within understandings of how people learn to read and write and the ways that literacy affects one's position in society.

MY STORIES OF PRISON

While professionally I care about the topic of justice-involved people and formerly incarcerated women's education, I have a personal connection to the research as well. The story that is closest to me is the story of family members who have been incarcerated. One story in particular stands out as coloring how I see imprisonment, our criminal justice system, as well as other issues regarding innocence, guilt, and shame. One family member, whom I will call Len, was in a state prison and considered innocent by everyone in my family. Len's incarceration was seen as unfair, the result of a dishonest witness's testimony, and a broken justice system. Money was given to Len from members of the family to help with lawyers' fees; even so, Len was prosecuted and imprisoned. As a young girl, my interactions with Len were filled with their kindness, generosity, humor, and lightheartedness. Len's conviction, trial, and imprisonment occurred when I was a teen, and while everyone in the family believed in Len's innocence, the incarceration was rarely discussed openly. It was clear to me that while we believed Len was wrongly convicted, the imprisonment itself was considered shameful. When I was in my early twenties, I accompanied three generations of my extended family, as we traveled many miles and crowded into two adjoining hotel rooms for one particular visit with Len. I remember on that visit, I sensed Len had changed. The lighthearted joking that was once a constant with Len now had a bitter edge to it. Len, a middle-class college graduate who had been married with children and employed by a prestigious business, had become quite different during the incarceration. Len was released and has battled chronic physical illnesses since that time. At the same time, Len has also developed a zealousness for all things spiritual and religious.

I experienced Len's story through the eyes of a child, teen, and young adult, and it colored my understanding of what it means to be a person involved in the criminal justice system. It affected how I see guilt, shame, punishment, truth, and so many other concepts that are tightly entwined in our criminal justice system. I saw firsthand how incarceration affects immediate and extended family members. In writing this preface, I realized that I had no idea how long Len had served. I was able to look up on the state corrections website to find out they were convicted to five to seven years and served three years and six months.

At the same time, while I come from a middle-class white family, I have known many of the circumstances which often accompany female victimization, crime, and incarceration. Addiction, mental illness, and abuse were realities I grew up seeing, and these resulted in unhealthy behaviors in my young adulthood. I am painfully aware that the path I walked in my youth and young adulthood was similar to many women who are now incarcerated. Currently I teach a writing class at a medium/maximum security women's prison. I sometimes see myself in these women's eyes, and I feel a sort of survivor's guilt because we could easily have switched places. I could be her, and she could be me, if not for that wrong decision made or abandoned, if not for that helping hand extended or withdrawn.

The women in my creative writing class are at once like all other women even while their circumstances within the justice system are radically different. Through their writing, they use their voices to show their uniqueness and their humanity that can be swallowed up by the system in which they are rooted. In many ways they are like women anywhere else—at times funny and supportive, at other times backstabbing and bitter. But just when I think there is no difference between them and me, someone will say something to remind me just how different we are. Once I brought clementine oranges with me to the class, and I set the bag of them on the table when I arrived. After answering a barrage of questions,

"Who brought those?"
"Why did you bring them?"
"What are they for?"
"Can I have one?"
"Can I have more than one?"

the oranges disappeared from the table and I felt dizzy with the realization that something I took for granted—fresh fruit—was so unusual in this place. It became an item of suspicion and desire. I don't want to romanticize the lives of these women. I don't want to reinforce narratives that they are victims or helpless or evil. They are like all other women, but the prison where they live controls them in striking and loathsome ways. One woman confided in me that she was going to be released in twenty-one months, so she was working to prepare herself. She said to me, "I know it is different on the outside. I know this place is like being stuck in a snow globe." That image is one that I've rolled around in my head often, and I am struck by the simultaneous beauty and horror of that description. Everything inside the globe besides the snow itself is frozen in place, unable to interact with the beauty that floats around it. A snow globe also is a full picture that cannot be touched by the observer. It is enveloped in water and glass. I think of this image often when I consider the spatial aspects of prison, and when I consider how this is a permanent or semi-permanent reality for so many in the United States.

When I step through the prison gates on Tuesday evenings to teach my writing class, I realize I am a representative of the outside for my students while they carry the identity of incarcerated; when they sit in the classroom with me, they are also students, learners, and writers. I aim to help empower them through their writing, and I know that some of the writing they do and share has helped them better comprehend their past experiences and current realities.

MY STORIES OF STUDENTS

Beyond my own professional training, my experiences growing up, and all that I've learned teaching in a women's prison, to this research I also bring the stories of the students in my college writing classes. About six years ago I began noticing stories from some of my college students about their past incarcerations. Though I had taught over a decade, these stories were new to me, and as they became a bit more common, I started to pay closer attention. I was especially attentive because as any teacher knows, students choose carefully what details they share about themselves within classroom walls. These students were sharing stories about themselves that were an important part of their identities, but that they may not necessarily share with the rest of the world. There was a reason for the sharing, and I saw the sharing as gifts and signs that they felt safe to share that part of their identities. I recognized it as the same sort of gift I had given to a very few of my teachers as I was struggling to move through high school and then college. My own teachers' patient listening and belief in me is a gift I will forever work to repay.

Sometimes a prison story from one of my students came out as an aside. For example once a student asked if she could write her final research paper on voting rights of ex-felons because she wanted to be able to vote in the next presidential election. Sometimes, a student would make a sort of announcement to me after class or during office hours, a public owning of this identity, often apologetic, as an explanation of why he was not the best student, or why she was not getting the best grades.

When I began the interviews for this research study, I remember making small talk with one of the participants following our recorded interview, and I tried to put into words why I felt the need to do this research. Part of it, I said, was I wanted to understand my students better. But I also wanted to tell stories of those who were often ignored or erased. She said to me, "Melanie, we are invisible, but we are all around you. We are sitting in your classrooms. We are standing behind you in the grocery store checkout line. We are sitting across the aisle from you at a restaurant." And I was struck by how little we care or wonder or ask about this growing population of our sisters and brothers.

THE AIM AND HEART OF THE RESEARCH

This book, while stemming from my own interests in my students, is not a personal story. Although all qualitative research embeds the researcher within the research, I endeavor to use my interest in this topic to help shed light upon stories of those who are often invisible or voiceless. The research has been conducted through narrative inquiry, a particular form of narrative research which identifies story as a cognitive structure through which humans understand the world and their places within it. Therefore, my research was not so much about telling these women's stories as it was listening for and finding themes within the stories they used to explain their experiences.

The book is divided into two sections. Part I of the book corresponds with the initial research project which studied four formerly incarcerated women's storied literacy experiences before, during, and following incarceration. This first part of the book will show how across time, these women used and depended upon reading and writing to negotiate power, develop identities, and make sense of interpersonal connections. This section will include several chapters covering themes that emerged through the research, including the importance of prison libraries to incarcerated women's autonomy and identity formation; the literacy sponsorship of motherhood; and literacy sponsorship as markings of transition through trauma. The data set from this study includes narratives from individual interviews and email correspondence with the four formerly incarcerated women.

These four women, Grace, Lexi, Diane, and Becky,[1] shared stories of meaningful memories of literacy acts, letters written, Facebook messages, and library books, and these stories provided insights into the lived experiences of formerly incarcerated women and how they interacted and currently see themselves as interacting with reading and writing.

The second section is an extension of the first in that it continues the narrative research of one of the participants, Diane, as she narrates her experience transitioning from incarceration to college to graduation. This section includes data from multiple interviews with Diane, and interviews from three of her former professors and artifacts from her college classes.

Part II delves deeper into the storied experience of one individual's transition from incarceration at a state prison to becoming a university student, graduate, and writer, and the transitioning of her literacy experiences (both reading and writing) throughout that process. Overall, this book will connect the following threads: politically situated literacy; transitioning as storied processes dependent upon literacy sponsorship; and the lived experiences of formerly incarcerated women.

Because of the mass incarceration of individuals during the war on drugs, we have seen a great increase in our prison populations since the 1980s (Arditti 2012; DeRuy 2016; Reiter 2017). Many of these prisoners are now being released, and the numbers will affect and are affecting our communities. As the United States faces a growing population of justice-involved people stepping back into our communities, families, and schools, it is important to explore ways that these individuals can become successful through education and gaining or regaining cultural capital. This research aims to provide a small piece of that exploration, offered through the narratives of four very courageous women. Perhaps their stories will provide an understanding of both the promise and adversity faced by many others looking to reintegrate successfully. The stigma of justice-involved identities can paralyze or strangle. Perhaps in some small way these stories may initiate a loosening of stigma to allow deeper and more peaceful breathing.

NOTE

1. Names of all participants are pseudonyms selected by the participants themselves. All names of places and other individuals are also pseudonyms that were selected by the researcher.

Part I

Literate Acts and Narratives of Power Seized, Claimed, Relinquished, Denied

Chapter One

Stories and Sponsors

Narrative Inquiry and Literacy Sponsorship of Formerly Incarcerated Women

This chapter provides an overview of the research methodology and theoretical underpinnings of this study. Before detailing these in their complexities, I must explain that this research project was constructed first through the simple premise that justice-involved women experience oppression. Often the oppression they experience precludes, and leads inevitably to, their incarceration. One main purpose of prison is to correct through erasure, and this erasure of personhood is systemic and brutal. Through erasure and other acts of oppression which can be political, personal, cultural, or educational, women who are and have been involved in the criminal justice system must work through layers of destructive treatment in order to define themselves and overcome the erasure of their identities. Through acts of literacy, they in fact are able to create stories of their own identities that expand beyond and shatter the stigmatized stories placed upon them. Stories defining them as delinquent, thug, degenerate, victim, or casualty are all stigmas that justice-involved women live within and must overcome. Following incarceration, women carry these stories of their oppression with them beyond the prison gates, and the women in this study shared how the stories they were able to tell about themselves had the power to rupture stigmas, and provided constructive and empowering identities. This study does not assume an uncomplicated picture of a correctional system that "corrects" or prisoners who become "rehabilitated" in the simplest terms of the words. Rather, this study begins with the premise that any correction or rehabilitation results from an oppressive political mechanism that in many cases is merely an accessory of justice-involved women's pre- and post-prison lives. These premises become more sinister and compounded within the staggering statistics of female mass incarceration in the United States.

In general, the United States has a prison problem. The country has five percent of the world's population, but 20 percent of the world's population of incarcerated people (US Department of Education 2016). In 2001 the United States held a record of 1.3 million people in prisons (Visher and Travis 2003); and at the time that this book is being written, there are 840,000 parolees and 3.6 million people on probation (Sawyer and Wagner 2019). Since 1990, combined state and federal funding for higher education has not increased at all, while spending on prisons and jails has increased 89 percent (US Department of Education 2016). The increase in the prison population has also seen disparate growth in male versus female populations. Within 2000-2015, the rate of women incarcerated rose 50 percent, a surprisingly higher rate than the rise in male incarcerated (18%) (Walmsley 2016), resulting in distinct and destructive social consequences since most of these women are mothers and family caretakers.

While it is expensive and arguably immoral to imprison this many people, there are further complications involved in the long-term and generational results of mass incarceration. Almost all people who are currently incarcerated will one day be released and reintegrate into our communities. We must consider the lessons they have learned while imprisoned. Are these lessons of despair and suspicion, lessons of silence and obliteration, or lessons of control and subjugation? One premise of this study is that education in general and literacy education in particular provides insight and assistance as formerly incarcerated people are woven or rewoven into our communities in healthy, constructive, and truly rehabilitative ways.

Research conclusively points to several possibilities to reduce recidivism, and two of these possibilities are intrinsically intertwined and also key to understanding the importance of this study. First, research has shown that education affects crime and recidivism. Lochner and Moretti (2004) identified that an investment in education provides a social economic benefit related to crime and incarceration. Economic savings result from funding education by saving money in policing and incarceration. Other studies have shown unequivocally that educational programs within prison reduce recidivism (Davis et al. 2013; US Department of Education 2016; Bender 2018). While around 40 percent of prisoners will return to prison within three years of release, those prisoners who were involved in a prison education program are 43 percent less likely to return to prison (Opsal 2011). It bears to reason that educated prisoners are more likely to find employment following release.

In addition, research shows that formerly incarcerated women in particular who are able to develop identities beyond that of criminal or victim are able to disrupt negative social expectations and restory their experiences in positive ways, allowing them to have more successful reentry experiences (Opsal 2011). General prison education programs allow prisoners to develop identities as students, workers, learners, and other more productive roles beyond the socially defined prisoner identity. Literacy education in particular provides a more complex humanistic identity as justice-involved students begin to imagine and negotiate new life pathways through reading and create new identities and self-expression through writing (Lockard and Rankins-Robertson 2018).

Beyond recidivism of all formerly incarcerated people, it is important to consider women in particular because of the impact they have on families and children (Arditti 2012; Ferraro and Moe 2003; Willison and O'Brien 2017). Education and literacy as issues surrounding female criminality, incarceration, and recidivism are not just moral issues but logical ones as they can benefit generations of individuals and the whole of society (Arditti 2012; Willison and O'Brien 2017; Bender 2018).

I would be remiss to not also include a discussion of race. As many scholars have pointed out, the prison industrial complex should be considered racist; the majority of incarcerated people are Black, (Heitzeg 2009; Alexander 2012; McTier et al. 2017; St. John and Blount-Hill 2019). Scholars have also identified the school to prison pipeline and have clearly shown how Black and Latinx children most often attend schools that mimic the culture and assumptions of the criminal justice system; these children then are socialized to become justice-involved adults (Wald and Losen 2003; Heitzeg 2009; Alexander 2012). This study's participants are white and Latinx, and do not represent the general population-incarcerated people. They also all have obtained a high school diploma or GED. According to Eleanor Novek (2019), in 2010, 55.7 percent of incarcerated people had not graduated high school, and 61.8 percent of Black incarcerated people did not have a high school diploma (55). Therefore, these women in the study have obtained literacy and educational levels within the upper half of the general population of incarcerated people.

This was a consideration throughout the study and the participants can provide us with an understanding of the lived experiences of formerly incarcerated white and Latinx women, and all formerly incarcerated women to a small extent. However, there are clear in pointing out the limitations. These women (especially the three white women) carry privilege and social currency that comes from their skin color. The majority of justice-involved women do not hold these advantages. While the stories told through this study's participants' experiences can certainly inform us, it is crucial to remember the challenges faced by most formerly incarcerated women are further complicated and formidable because of the systematic racism they must also face.

THE NEED FOR EXPANDED SCHOLARSHIP

There have been a number of recent studies focused on correctional education (Appleman 2019; Berry 2018; Custer 2016; Davis et al. 2013; Ginsburg 2019; Halcovic 2014; Halcovic and Greene 2015; Jones and Manger 2019; McTier et al. 2017; Patterson 2018; Rogers et al. 2017), and some scholarship has focused upon education and literacy of incarcerated women (Arditti 2012; Brown and Bloom 2018; Cobbina and Bender 2012; Curry and Jacobi 2017; Hinshaw and Jacobi 2015; Jacobi and Stanford 2014; Sweeney 2010). Even so, the argument can be made that there is still a great need to better understand lived experiences, identity, literacy, and educational transitions of justice-involved women. In many ways, Reiter describes prison research can be "pixelated" and "providing a blurry view" (2014, 417) and needs to be brought into focus in order not only to understand and resolve the problems connected to mass incarceration, but also to decrease rates of recidivism and support positive reentry of formerly incarcerated women. Incarceration aims to erase and contain the criminal, and in this action, the specifics surrounding the realities of corrections are often obscured or concealed as well. Researchers have recently called for more holistic research that could help expose the realities of mass incarceration (Reiter 2014; Visher and Travis 2003; Willison and O'Brien 2017). Others have called for more gendered research (Curry and Jacobi 2017; Ferraro and Moe 2003; Hinshaw and Jacobi 2015; Willison and O'Brien 2017) to better understand how formerly incarcerated women can integrate successfully into society. We need more research focused in particular upon women's education, before, during and after incarceration, and especially how this education can be utilized to move beyond the stigmatized identities of criminal, victim, or inmate.

This study aimed to answer three interconnected questions regarding literacy practices and incarceration of women. These questions were, first, what are storied literacy experiences of formerly incarcerated women across time including before, during, and following incarceration? Second, who or what have been the literacy sponsors of formerly incarcerated women? And finally, how can prison education programs better sponsor literacies of formerly incarcerated women? This study is centered purposefully upon formerly incarcerated women because of the major increase in female incarceration in the last decade, and also because many studies on justice-involved people's education is focused upon recidivism and identifies males as the primary participants. The intention here is to clarify and bring to light truths within what could be argued an even more "pixelated" area of prison experience through the stories of formerly incarcerated women.

THEORETICAL FRAMEWORK

Literacy is a particularly important aspect of education because of the ways reading and writing can provide social and cultural access. Since the 1980s, literacy studies have taken a social turn through which reading and writing have been identified as politically wrought acts (Gee 2015; Friere and Macedo 1987; New London Group 1996). Through reading and writing, we can position ourselves within a social framework or find ourselves positioned by others. Literacy can empower when it is used to critique, define, reflect upon, and explore one's realities. A flexibility of communication within many discourse communities and comprehension of discourses within multiple contexts provides an individual more social freedom, power, and access. Freire explained it in this way, "Reading the world always precedes reading the word, and reading the word implies continually reading the world. . . . In a way, however, we can go further and say that reading the word is not preceded merely by reading the world, but by a certain form of writing it or rewriting it, that is, of transforming it by means of conscious, practical work" (Freire and Macedo 1987, 35). In other words, the reading and writing people do in life affects their social capital, their perception of reality, as well as others' perceptions of them; they also affect one's ability or lack thereof to move freely and advantageously within multiple social frameworks. The social framework of an incarcerated woman is defined often by her crime or the stigma that comes with an inmate identity. Her punishment extends following her release through clear legal boundaries created for continued surveillance and control. Her punishment also extends through more invisible, but equally real stigmas that aim to demarcate who she can become. The ability to read other worlds and write beyond the reality created for her, allows a formerly incarcerated woman to take some control back from the grand narratives encircling and constraining her.

Literacy Sponsorship of Formerly Incarcerated Women

Deborah Brandt, while identifying and extending literacy as a social practice that is both local and global, theorized the phrase *Sponsors of Literacy* as "any agents, local or distant, concrete or abstract, who enable, support, teach, model, as well as recruit, regulate, suppress, or withhold literacy—and gain advantage by it in some way" (Brandt 1998, 166). Deborah Brandt also identified the term *folding in* as the extension of human literacy sponsors to nonhuman objects or entities that allow or constrain literate acts (Brandt and Clinton 2002, 53). Nonhuman sponsors of literacy could be entities or phenomena such as computer access, prison libraries, or even international travel. Literacy learning, in Brandt's theory, is not a process that takes place solely within the walls of a school. Brandt observed literacy sponsorship existing in technologies, spaces, as well as in people. She further identified constructive and destructive sponsors of literacy. Constructive sponsors are those that create positive growth in literacy practices or skills, those that "enable, support, teach, model." Conversely, destructive sponsors influence negative results from their sponsorship; in Brandt's words, they "regulate, suppress, or withhold literacy." Brandt's research is also based upon the assumption that literacy is political and creates or denies paths of power and identity within a culture.

These understandings of literacy as socially constructed and politically fraught can also be used in identifying the absence of literate acts, for example when books or writing utensils are withheld in a prison, or when a student chooses not to participate in a lesson or assignment. These absences of literacy enact specific negotiations of control and agency, and as Kirk Branch describes, the power may lie in the absence. "This power of literacy—not to change positively the cultures or people who become literate or enact practices that challenge domination, but to control, label, punish, deprive, and limit access—serves a critical function for managing both educational and social systems" (Branch 2009, 55). The withholding of literacy from a prisoner is a part of a larger destructive literacy sponsorship wrapped up in the silencing and controlling punishment of US corrections systems. A student refusing to participate could be seen negatively as lacking motivation or intelligence. On the other hand, this action could also be seen as the student exerting control over her own literacy and acting against dominating practices of destructive literacy sponsors which are working to indoctrinate or control her.

Sponsors of literacy, then, for justice-involved women, can be constructive or destructive, and are always political in nature, and markers of power and control. The presence or absence of literacy acts or sponsorship influences one's sense of autonomy and control, thereby significantly affecting an incarcerated woman's constructive identity formation, cultural capital, and social autonomy, all of which are related to the likelihood of positive reentry or recidivism. The literacy acts and absences that are inherent to prisons, therefore, position the very ecology and geography of a correctional institution as a destructive literacy sponsor while it regulates and suppresses an incarcerated person's literacy and literate acts. Because formerly incarcerated women have experienced such an intense and destructive sponsorship, this study is undergirded in the theoretical stance that participants are working through and within experiences of political, personal, and educational oppression, some of which occurred before incarceration and many of which occurred during and after their imprisonment.

Feminist Theory of Incarceration/Criminology

Within the field of criminal justice there are theories of how women become criminals and then incarcerated. Originally, female models of criminology were based upon models of men's experiences. Women who participated in criminal behavior were deemed deviant, immoral, and evil. More recent models are from feminist positioning which acknowledges women's life experiences are expressly different from men's because of multiple layers of power differentials and oppression. Through a more feminist lens have come theories which identify structures and processes that most likely influence women to become involved in criminal behavior. Hagan's power control theory (1989) helped envision criminality as a gendered process and socialized experience that was in part dependent upon social structures and contexts. Hagan contended that through patriarchal or more egalitarian family structures, men and women grow up socialized in different ways. These power differentials influence one's likelihood of exhibiting aggressive or criminal behaviors. Of course, this theory relies upon a two-parent family structure, and if viewing criminal behavior through power control theory, one must take into consideration the power variances that a single parent or divorced parent family structure may initiate. Life course theory (Sampson and Laub 1995) identifies adolescence as the crucial period when many criminal behaviors may be developed. This theory also provides the explanation that there are certain socially acceptable life events and activities that provide protective influences. Others have added gendered experiences to life course theory and looked at how such life experiences such as marriage, an impoverished childhood, or consistent employment may provide stability or instability that impacts drug addiction and other criminal pathways (Thompson and Petrovic 2009; Estrada and Nilsson 2012; Wright et al. 2013).

Certainly all contemporary theories of incarcerated women and gendered criminology work from the standpoint that there are socially constructed and gendered roles that define what acceptable female behavior looks like. These accepted standards are dependent upon masculine power and affect women throughout their lifespans. When women exhibit socially defined aberrant behaviors, or if they resist abusive patriarchal systems, punishment results in various forms. If they are unable to physically escape these same abusive systems, many women turn to escapist behaviors, such as drug abuse, that in turn open doors to more serious criminal behavior. Female criminology cannot be viewed outside the power dynamics of gendered oppression and exploitation. This study uses this lens as one of the starting points for understanding the ways that formerly incarcerated women negotiate various sites of power, including how they use or are denied access to literacy and education.

METHODOLOGY

The purpose of the study was to collect and analyze storied literacy experiences of formerly incarcerated women. Stories of reading and writing, both in and out of school, were collected through interviews and emails. The study used narrative inquiry (Connelly and Clandinin 1990; Clandinin and Connelly 2000) as its methodology. The study also incorporated feminist research methodologies (Smith 1987; Olesen 1994; Smith 2013) to better capture and explore the lived experiences of participants.

Narrative Inquiry

Narrative inquiry, when used, also always serves as a theoretical framework. In this study, narrative inquiry, together with Deborah Brandt's (1998) theories of literacy sponsors, and theories of literacy as social practice (New London Group 1996; Brandt and Clinton 2002; Gee 2014) served as theoretical frames. The appearances and absences of literacy sponsors in participants' narratives were identified and analyzed.

Narrative has taken different forms in qualitative research, and in particular the fields of education and women's studies, because of the multifaceted way the methodology can capture and relate complexities of experience. There are two main uses of narrative in qualitative research: *narrative analysis* and *narrative inquiry*, and differentiation between the two here is necessary in order to clearly depict the data collection and coding that took place. Narrative analysis represents story as a discursive action (Gergen and Gergen 2006), not necessarily a research methodology. Through narrative analysis, the qualitative data is collected in diverse ways, and then it is analyzed through narrative elements such as a traditional plot structure, character, setting, and conflict. In this way, the data is presented and made sense of through storied representations created by the researcher.

Narrative inquiry on the other hand was used in this study and takes a pointedly different stance. Clandinin and Connelly (2000) identified narrative inquiry as a unique methodology of doing qualitative research. Within this methodology, story is seen as a cognitive structure within which participants comprehend and portray their experience. The assumption is that humans understand reality through the storying and restorying of it, and this storying controls and reveals our perception of experience, identity, ambition, and history. Researchers who undertake narrative inquiry collect participant stories as data. Interview questions often request the sharing of stories. In particular, researchers consider a larger, three-dimensional, narrative landscape which participants create and engage in. This landscape's dimensions are temporality, sociality, and spatiality. Temporality is particularly important and captured within this study because participants were asked to share literacy stories before, during, and after incarceration. Sociality was observed within the data through notation of relationships with literacy sponsors and was distinguished further by identification of constructive and destructive literacy sponsors. Spatiality was significant because some collected stories were set within prison walls, where space was limited, defined, and controlled in very poignant ways. Finally, narrative inquiry identifies story as a theoretical position rather than a coding or reporting device. It is within this theoretical position where the researcher and participants can convene and work to identify and contemplate storied experience.

The methodology of narrative inquiry was taken up in this study in response to the guidance of Hinshaw and Jacobi (2015), who encouraged a more feminist methodological stance when considering the writing of incarcerated women. Their evidence showed how some methodologies reinforced the "spectacle" of the incarcerated woman and fortified incarcerated women's identities primarily through their crimes. Hinshaw and Jacobi called for more authentic voices. This study's methodology was designed to answer their call and resist popular socially constructed portrayals of formerly incarcerated women. Incarceration within this study is both a temporal and spatial marker of experience, but it does not identify the participants through their crimes. Incarceration is portrayed as one experience among many. Further, narrative inquiry was selected because the researcher's stance during data collection is as a collector rather than the creator of stories. Researchers within narrative inquiry do not "story" the experiences for participants, and are methodologically cognizant to not colonize the participants' narratives.

Positionality of Narrative Researchers: Narrative Inquiry/Methodology

Within the process of narrative inquiry, the researcher is not an impartial outsider researching the subject from afar. In fact, the process of narrative inquiry fully rejects the assumption that a researcher can be objective or somehow step out of her own narratives and into a storyless framework. This is one reason that I chose to begin this book with a description of some of the stories and experiences I bring to this project. Within the three-dimensional landscape identified by Clandinin and Connelly, the researcher is an active participant. In fact, they state that researchers engaging in narrative inquiry "are not merely objective inquirers, people on the high road, who study a world lesser in quality than our moral temperament would have it, people who study a world we did not help create. On the contrary, we are complicit in the world we study . . . we work in the space not only with our participants but also with ourselves" (Clandinin and Connelly 2000, 61). A researcher working within this methodology is never a mere recorder of narratives. The narratives are said to be "constructed" and "co-constructed" narrative tellings through which she engages with the subject and the storying within a specific time, context and relationship.

As I designed and engaged in this research, I kept reflective notes inter-mittently to help me process the ways I was viewing the participants' stories and identify where I may have been unconsciously projecting my own story-ing. These reflective notes were read before the coding process and analysis of research texts. While Clandinin and Connelly remind researchers, "We are in the parade we assume to study" (2000, 81), reflective notes and other processes can help researchers identify where they march within the parade, and understand next to whom they are marching, and if the music they march to is mainly from other musicians, or their own drumbeat.

The self-reflective stance of narrative inquiry is complementary to the other piece of this research project's design, that of feminist methodology. These theories can be interconnected, and several researchers have identified feminist narrative research as a methodology that carries the potential of providing an especially rich contextual lens in understanding the lived expe-riences of women especially as it is highly reflexive and focused upon issues of power and oppression (Woodiwiss et al. 2017). The following specific feminist research assumptions were taken up in this project:

- Researchers should identify and acknowledge how they are intrinsically interwoven into the research.
- Research should purposefully aim to identify and oppose engendered power structures.
- Gender affects experience and therefore colors participant data.
- An important aim of research is to uncover diversity in human experience rather than assume there is one objective experiential truth to uncover.

Especially pertinent to the methodology and philosophical framework of this study is the work of Dorothy Smith (1987), who identified women's experi-ence and research as dependent upon one's particular standpoint, and each standpoint is dependent upon socially constructed power differentials. In addition, framing this study is the work of Linda Tuhiwai Smith (2013) and her explanations of how the researcher's gaze inherently others the partici-pant, and socially just research should aim for a more reflexive relationship between studier and studied. The researcher should study her own positional-ity, especially her position in relationship to the study's participants. Some of the processes and procedures used to enact these theories are as follows in Table 1.1:

Table 1.1.   Feminist Research Methods

Location in Study	Feminist Process or Procedure
In Design	• Interview questions were open-ended and lightly structured to allow for participants to take the conversation where they wanted and provide an authentic storying of their experiences. • Narrative specifically was used in an attempt to uncover the unique, layered, and varied experiences of participants. • I did not include questions regarding where or why participants were incarcerated. No experiences of crime or abuse or addiction were requested. Instead, the questions focused upon participants' experiences with reading and writing throughout their lives, with incarceration merely serving as a chronological marker.
Before Data Collection	• I shared questions with participants prior to the interviews to allow them time to consider and claim the experiences they wished to share.
During Data Collection	• I was in contact with each participant following the research interview, requesting any follow-up material, memories, stories that the participant might remember following the interview, allowing a flexibility in participant response.
Through Analysis	• I carefully built and adhered to a process of analysis that demanded I identify my own storying and acknowledge how my stories interacted with the stories of the participants. In this way, I worked to break down the imperialistic stance of researcher upon researched. • In the analysis, I depended upon the participants' own words found within transcripts and written documents.

Participants

This study's participants were four formerly incarcerated women who were currently living in the midwestern United States, and who all came from different small towns or medium-sized cities. All personal names are pseudonyms selected by the participants. All names of other individuals and places or programs are also pseudonyms. I asked participants to self-identify gender, race, age, and length of incarceration. Though I did not ask for these details, during the interview process, all women also mentioned their children, their levels of education, and their employment.

Lexi was the youngest of the participants. At the time of the interview, she was twenty-eight, and a white female. She had two daughters, one of whom she had before being incarcerated and the other following her incarceration. She was incarcerated for four years and eleven months. She had graduated from high school but had not attended college. She was employed and in a relationship with her daughters' father.

Grace was forty-six and identified as Latina. She was incarcerated for three years and two months. She had five children before she was incarcerated. She had completed high school but had not attended college. She was employed full time, and she did not mention a spouse or partner.

Diane was forty-nine and a white female. She was incarcerated for five years. She was married and had six children from a previous relationship before her incarceration. She and her husband owned their own tree-service business. She had a bachelor's degree in English that she earned following her incarceration and she mentioned that she had considered attending graduate school.

Becky identified as a white female in her fifties. She was incarcerated for nine years. She was single and had two daughters who were born before her incarceration. Though she described a number of educational programs she had completed including Job Corps and other vocational or technical education programs during her incarceration, she earned a GED while she was incarcerated, but did not graduate from high school. She was not employed at the time of the interview; she was living on disability funding and struggled with several health issues.

Participants were recruited through the use of social media and posting recruitment requests around the campus where I worked. A total of twelve individuals originally contacted me and agreed to take part in this study. Over the course of the data collection period, though, many of those recruited were unable to participate or withdrew from the study. Certainly, it is often complicated to secure participation in qualitative research; however, this population was especially challenging to recruit. Over the course of the study, some participants who had agreed to interviews would then be unavailable, means of contact would be cut off, or participants would fail to attend designated interview appointments. The participants were not compensated for their participation, except they were offered a meal that took place during the interview process. This lack of compensation may have affected the recruitment numbers, but this also suggests the four participants were sincere in their desires to share their experiences and to share them unreservedly. The choice to not provide compensation was an ethical decision based upon the desire to have participants who elected freely to share their stories, without expectation of payoff, and to not persuade participation through financial or material reward. This was also based upon the discussions of doing research with justice-involved people and formerly incarcerated women (Rogers, Hinshaw, Holding, and Jacobi 2017; Wesely 2018) and the care researchers must take while working with these populations who have been so influenced to perform in certain ways by outside rewards and punishments.

Before meeting with each participant, I asked whether she would like to have questions sent to her through regular mail or email. Per each participant's preference, a list of interview questions was sent through email for review. Questions were open-ended and did not include language regarding literacy sponsorship or language that focused questions upon literacy experiences that "helped" or "hindered." This enabled data to be analyzed through both inductive and deductive methods. Interview questions were worded to collect narratives of different times in the participants' lives focused upon reading and writing, and they were structured to include probes that would encourage more description and details in the narratives. The interview protocol was organized into four sections, using similar questions in the first three sections. The first section was regarding experiences before incarceration, the second was during incarceration, and the third was following incarceration. The fourth section of the protocol requested that participants share their view of transition or change in literacy practices over time, and there was also the opportunity to describe any other stories that hadn't already been relayed. Questions often included a request for a story. Interview protocols are listed in Table 1.2.

The interview protocol specifically did not reference the participants' criminal activity or ask participants to divulge why they had been incarcerated. Protocol did not ask for specific personal information—for example, if the participants had children or partners, or if they were employed. Participants were also not asked to share the specifics of their educational background—for example, they were not asked if they finished high school or attended college or technical school. They also were not asked any questions in regard to current or past employment. These topics were consciously left out of the interview in order to allow participants space to craft their own stories of their literacy experiences before, during, and after incarceration. Therefore, the personal information that was connected to literacy narratives is pertinent and should be identified as connected closely to participant's understandings of who she is and was and will be regarding her reading and writing sponsorship and identity.

Though participants were not asked to divulge specifics about their educational background, it is clear that the women who participated employed literacy skills to the extent that they could correspond with the researcher through email, and the participants all had access to a computer or device with internet capabilities. The process of communication through email did likely constrict the participant pool, and one limitation of the study is that it did not include participants with a wide range of literacy skill levels.

Interviewing Processes

As Mishler (1991) contends, research participants naturally will use stories, just as people naturally use stories in their everyday conversations with each other. In traditional survey research interviewing, however, Mishler (1991) also notes that stories are often suppressed by the researcher (69) because stories cannot be quantified and can be difficult to code. In a traditional

Table 1.2.   Interview Protocol

Interview Section	Interview Protocol
Section 1: Pre-Incarceration Literacy Narratives	• Can you tell me a story of a time when you remember reading and/or writing growing up? This can be in or out of school, and for any purposes. • Can you share a story that shows opportunities that you had to read and write while growing up? • Why do you think this story is memorable? • Can you describe your feelings about reading and writing at this time? • What role models did you have to encourage reading and writing while growing up? Can you share any stories about them? • Can you remember any formal programs you were involved in growing up that included reading and writing? Can you share some memories about them? • Can you describe the places where you remember reading and writing? • Can you think of any other stories that you would like to share?
Section 2: Incarceration Literacy Narratives	• Can you tell me a story of a time when you remember reading and/or writing while incarcerated? This can be for any purposes. • Can you share a story that shows opportunities that you had to read and write while incarcerated? • Why do you think this story is memorable? • Can you describe your feelings about reading and writing at this time? • What role models did you have to encourage reading and writing while incarcerated? Can you share any stories about them? • Can you remember any formal programs you were involved in while incarcerated that included reading and writing? Can you share some memories about them? • Can you describe the places where you remember reading and writing? • Can you think of any other stories that you would like to share?

Section 3: **Post-** **Incarceration** **Literacy** **Narratives**	• Can you tell me a story of a time when you remember reading and/or writing during your reentry or following incarceration? • Why do you think this story is memorable? • Can you describe your feelings about reading and writing at this time? • What role models did you have to encourage reading and writing since your incarceration? Can you share any stories about them? • Are there any formal programs involving reading and writing that you are involved in now, or have been since incarceration? Can you share some memories about them? • Can you describe the places where you remember reading and writing during reentry and/or any time after incarceration? • Can you think of any other stories that you would like to share? Optional Question: • Can you share a story or stories that can show how your feelings toward reading and writing have changed or stayed the same over time?

interview, participants are often interrupted, to be kept "on topic." Following the suggestions of Mishler and others (Ellis and Berger 2003; Denzin and Lincoln 2005), attention was given to the researcher's assumptions of what stories should entail, and an interview protocol was created that invited stories possessing multiple interpretations.

Interviews ranged from thirty-five to ninety minutes depending upon how much each participant shared. Lexi, for example, was extremely succinct; she shared one or two brief stories per question and did not spend time elaborating without further probing questions from the researcher. Becky, however, spent over an hour and a half sharing stories and quoting Bible passages and poetry. Interviews took place in public spaces but were situated to provide some privacy for the participants' descriptions. Interviews were audio-recorded and transcribed. Following each interview, the researcher emailed the participant thanking her for her help and requested that if the participant remembered anything else relevant, to please send any memories in an email. Diane and Becky communicated with the researcher through email following the interviews, but Grace and Lexi did not.

As with any qualitative research process, the researcher obtains data through their personal biases and frameworks. To acknowledge and negotiate this stance, I wrote reflective field notes following each interview based upon three strategies identified by Clandinin, Connelly, and Chan (2002) in their recommendations for data collection in narrative inquiry. The first strategy is Recovery of Meaning, which is a basic summary of events and data in which the researcher reads the experience "from the inside . . . uncritically." The second strategy is Reconstruction of Meaning, which is a personal response, and a reading "from [the researcher's] own intentions" using "biases to generate possibilities." Here biases are clearly acknowledged and in fact used to clarify the positioning of the researcher. Finally, the third strategy is Reading at the Boundaries, which is a critique of the experience. This is a reading "at the interface between the text [the data, the experience] and the formalistic and reductionistic boundaries" (Clandinin et al. 2002, 133). These strategies allowed the layered processing of data through field notes as a self-reflective interval between data collection and analysis.

ANALYSIS AND RESULTS

The interview protocol was structured to invite the production of narratives, but it did not allow for a more in-depth life history analysis. The questions were framed to evoke narratives of reading and writing in any form, purpose or extent. The process of data analysis in narrative inquiry follows coding which is closely linked to narrative as a form of thinking and writing. Therefore, the field and research texts were also coded through increasingly complex viewings of how stories overlap or intersect with other stories. There were interim research texts which described or reflected upon common story lines. These also began to portray where silences, grand narratives, and counternarratives became visible through the revisions and negotiations of stories. This movement from field to research text is described by Clandinin and Connelly (2000) as looking for the "patterns, narrative threads, tensions and themes either within or across an individual's experience and in the social setting" (132).

Analysis took place through multiple steps to better understand layers of participants' experiences. A priori codes were taken from the work of Brandt. Therefore, the first codes were to identify sponsors described in the data, and then to further identify each sponsor as either a constructive or destructive sponsor of literacy. Once the sponsors were identified within the data, emergent codes were identified across participants' identification of sponsorship. Themes emerged regarding the spaces, situations, and consequences of sponsorship within participants' lives. Sponsorships were then categorized within these emergent codes of mothering, transitioning, and prison libraries and librarians. The chapters included in part I describe these findings and are further outlined below.

OVERVIEW OF PART I

The results of this first phase of the research uncovered three important themes in participants' storying of their literacy experiences. Each of these themes is detailed in a corresponding chapter, and then the section ends with a concluding chapter which pulls together the three themes.

Chapter 2, entitled "Literacies of Transitioning, Power, and Owning the Story" describes how participants marked times of transition through their storying of certain literacy experiences. In narrative inquiry, transition is seen as nonlinear movement and subtle changes over a length of time rather than a moment of concrete, linear change. The women in this study each storied a literacy experience as a marker of transition. Through writing a letter, Grace narrated a mark of transition and empowerment over her abuser. Through the writing down and subsequent destruction of a notepad of memories, Diane narrated this as a longer transitional experience and a concrete signal of prevailing over her past. Becky described a series of messages she wrote which enabled her to change her reading of the past and its effect on her daughter. Her narrative included electronic messaging with her adult daughter, exploring memories of the night Becky was arrested. Within these messages, Becky was confronted by her daughter's lasting trauma, and in reaction she wrote a letter to another recipient which finally allowed her to process and take responsibility for how her experiences created lasting effects for those around her. Here, these women used literacy in constructive ways allowing them to self-advocate and write markers of transition.

Chapter 3, "'Because Our World Is Very Small': Prison Libraries and Librarians," is an overview of the many stories participants shared regarding their use of prison libraries and the relationships they had with prison librarians. Both libraries and librarians became powerful and constructive sponsors of literacy. The access to books provided identity formation, healing, and connection that was meaningful to the women while incarcerated and also to their transition when they were released. Prison librarians were described as important sponsors who saw the women's identities beyond their state of incarceration, but more positively as readers and thinkers.

Chapter 4, "Mothering through Literate Acts: Facebook, Texts, and 'My Happiest Thing Ever,'" recounts participants' stories of literacy experiences connected to their identities as mothers. At times the women identify children as constructive sponsors of their literacy. Uniquely, one participant, Lexi, identifies herself as an important sponsor to her daughters' successful literacy development. Throughout the narratives, participants connect literacy and mothering to circumvent and complicate the negative roles of inmate, criminal, or victim which have been placed upon them through their incarceration.

Finally, chapter 5, "Three-Dimensional Landscapes of Formerly Incarcerated Women's Literacy Narratives," provides an overview of findings from the study and expands commentary regarding new questions that have emerged through this study as well as implications for future research.

The second half of this book follows chapter 5 and includes chapters 6 through 10. This part II, entitled "Layered Narratives and Sponsorships: Diane's Prison to College Identities," provides a continuation of the study overviewed in part I and delivers an in-depth inquiry into Diane's experience as a college student following her incarceration.

Chapter Two

Literacies of Transitioning, Power, and Owning the Story

One of the afflictions of incarceration is the appearance that life comes to a standstill. However, despite appearances, life never pauses, and in narrative inquiry especially, there is an acknowledgement of constant motion and movement throughout time, community, and space. Clandinin and Connelly remind us that "narratives are also always within a matrix of becoming" (2000), and through time, a person's stories change and become new. In many ways, a justice-involved person's humanity disappears, yet through the act of reading and writing, an incarcerated or formerly incarcerated woman can make her humanity visible and extend her imagination beyond the walls of her circumstances and stigma. Many describe the experience of reading and writing as the ability to inhabit many lives at once, an extension of one's humanity. The women in this study portrayed many contradictory experiences, including the feeling of being simultaneously contained and freed, of being stigmatized and provided with possibilities. They described experiences of being emptied, invisible, and destroyed while simultaneously sharing stories of empowerment, resistance, and self-advocacy. Often these contradictory narratives pointed to times of transition, and portrayed extremes in mental or physical movement.

In narrative inquiry, transition is identified differently from the conventional conceptions of this word. While transition traditionally implies "an abruptness and certainty of change with a focus on the two ends of the process, the endpoint of one state and the onset of the next" (Clandinin et al. 2013, 219), understanding narratives of lives in transition includes the assumption that a transitional plotline is often created in response to a "normal" or institutionalized plotline. These transitional plotlines can also become counternarratives and portray webs of relationships (Clandinin et al. 2013), which occur within concrete spaces, and exist not as abrupt, definite change but instead as gradual movements through time. Counternarratives exist within contexts of power differentials wherein the counternarrative represents a suppression of true lived experience that differed from the socially constructed and accepted grand narrative. Transitional narratives, when moving away from the grand narrative, move and develop gradually, in a slow unfastening from the grand narrative. At times it may seem to be in agreement with the grand narrative while ultimately opposing it.

Clandinin et al. (2013) identified four qualities of a narrative understanding of transition. First, as previously stated, transition through a narrative lens takes place through gradual shifts and movements rather than a sudden change. While the common nomenclature of transition is used to identify a single turning away from or toward something new, in narrative understandings, transition is rarely a singular turning. The turning is not a sudden sweep, but rather there are invisible movements, subtle at first, containing doubts, starts and stops, hesitation, delaying and wavering before there is ever a visible resolution or clear movement toward change. So, too, following what seems to be certainty is actually a slight looking back, reflecting, wondering and insecurity before the transition can be identified as solid and complete. Second, all of life and all narrative views of life are in continual movement and flux. There is no such thing as a life that is fully stagnant, and while on the outside one may seem to be in a stable or motionless, unchanging state, narrative portrays the true depiction of constant movement that occurs within space, relationships, and over time, within one's perceptions. The internal narration of one's past and future selves, and how these affect the storying and restorying of one's present, is in a constant state of conversation and change. Third, transitional spaces within narrative research are envisioned as liminal spaces and can inhabit all areas of a position simultaneously. A transition, then, in narrative imagining, is not a linear movement over a threshold. Rather, it is a space where one resides upon, over, and within the threshold for a time, providing freedom and unsteadiness to create and select the narrative chronology. Finally, the fourth quality of narrative understanding of transition is that transition is always made up of improvisation. The liminal spaces of transition, therefore, are spaces of uncertainty but also spaces of power where an individual may move from within the accepted, dominant narrative to invent, improvise, and design her own story. Indeed, the act of writing allows the author to concretely see her own narrative movement and transition even while improvising within this very liminal space.

Participants in this study narrated literacy experiences as markers of transitional phases in their lives. A piece of writing, a letter, or an email, created concrete markers of invisible or subtle series of changes. The act of putting something into writing provides a permanence to the text that signifies and perhaps simplifies something that is larger taking place over an expanse of time, through relationships, and covering multiple spaces. These literacy experiences also portrayed transition by marking where a participant's lived experiences conflicted with or even broke away from the existing dominant institutional and social narratives. An instant message conversation on Face-book or a text message dialogue is not as fleeting as a conversation because it is written down. These written texts, letters, emails become permanent records that a reader can go back to, ponder, and either reject or fold into her existing narrative. Here too, these written conversations, both composed and read, can become important visible markers of transition, creating concrete permanent records of narrative movement which may otherwise be so gradu-al as to be invisible.

During the interview process, participants were never asked to describe transitional times in their lives. The words "change" or "transition" were never used in the interview protocol (see list of interview protocol in chapter 1). When asked to share stories of important memories of reading and writ-ing, participants identified literacy experiences which were then identified through the data analysis as storied markers of transition. Grace told the story of an important letter she wrote as a marker of her own power to break away from the dangerous, abusive narrative she inhabited as a child and teenager. Diane described writing out her memories as a way to overcome past abuse and move beyond trauma. Becky described a conversation with her daughter on Facebook which marked her mental transition to admit guilt for her past. This changed how Becky narrated both her past and future and how she narrated her relationship with her daughter.

From the very beginnings of educational theory, reflection is accepted as a way to organize and learn from experiences (Dewey 1997; James 1983). Mezirow (1990) identified critical reflection as an act that transformed the adult learner in particular because it provided adults with the ability to ques-tion and in turn reinforce or change past patterns of behavior, assumptions, and experience. Author Flannery O'Conner said, "I write because I don't know what I think until I read what I say." In his book *On Writing Well*, William Zinsser said, "writing is thinking on paper." Novelist E. M. Forster said, "How can I know what I think until I see what I say?" It is a common understanding among professional writers and writing teachers that the act of writing clarifies and crystalizes one's thoughts. Some authors have claimed all writing to be a form of autobiography wherein the act of writing allows clarification of one's true self upon the page (Murray 1991). If narrative transitioning truly is gradual, liminal, and improvisational, then the act of writing can make visible these varied and contradictory positions. Writing can provide a snapshot of this unstable operation of lived change, and be-cause of this, writing during these transitional times proved to be extremely poignant to participants. It allowed them to "think on paper" and see what narratives they were inhabiting when their lives were in an uncertain space of improvisation.

GRACE: WRITING TO ESCAPE HER ABUSER

When asked to share a story about an important memory of writing before incarceration, Grace immediately said she remembered writing notes and secretly passing them to her friends in school, but she didn't remember much about what was written in these notes. A follow-up question, asking if there were any letters or notes in which the content was memorable, she described in detail a letter she wrote as a teenager and the context surrounding it. The letter was to her father, who was also her abuser. In the letter she told him she was leaving home. Grace said she placed the letter in an envelope addressed to her father, and she left it for him while he slept. Then she snuck out of the house in the middle of the night. She described it in this way: "The day I left home, when I was eighteen, I wrote a goodbye letter to my dad. It was very nasty. Just to my dad because he was very abusive, and I had to run away." The narrative quality defined as the liminal space of transition (Clandinin et al. 2013) is clear here as Grace describes a close connection through the need to say goodbye to her abuser, and at the same time the need to leave a "nasty" letter in which she identifies his abuse and names him as an abuser: "I know that I probably told him, 'you're done putting your hands on me, and you're done doing things to me that daddies don't do to little girls. I'm out.'"

While Grace identified writing this letter as an important literacy memory, she explained that the importance was in the act of writing it and leaving it, knowing her father would finally read her point of view. The writing and leaving of the letter also forced her to act, and consequently moved her narrative forward into a new space. Once the letter was left and read, it would be difficult to stay or even to return home. While Grace had suffered and contemplated leaving for some time, the letter placed a marker in the transition of Grace's leaving and changed the liminal space to one of action.

Grace also explained that after her leaving, the letter was never mentioned in her family. While it provided momentum for Grace's physical transition away from her abuser, it did not work as an impetus for healing of relationships or further conversation. When asked what her father's response was to the letter, Grace explained that he never responded, but she knew he read it, and she assumed her mother did as well. It remained a silent symbol of Grace's leaving. Grace said she knew he read it only because the envelope had been opened, "He kept it for years. My mom still has it. They kept it, and he kept it where I left it. He read it—[I know] he opened it, 'cause I sealed it." The breaking of the seal identified his reading of her message. And the fact that the opened letter was left where Grace had placed it could be a rejection of Grace's narrative of leaving as well as her proclamation of abuse and escape. The opening but not moving of the letter and the silence surrounding it became a symbol of how Grace's and her parents' narratives of their relationships had been broken. The permanence of the message—that Grace would no longer allow his abuse—was a physical claim of a crime and Grace's rejection of her victimization. The letter held more power than a conversation or an altercation. Since the letter was written out in one voice, of the abused, there was no opportunity for Grace's parents to contradict that narrative. Having left the opened letter upon the table where it was originally placed, made it a permanent though silent symbol in Grace's parents' home. Opening it, reading it, and then allowing it to sit where Grace had left it for him was both an acknowledgement and a devaluing of the words she wrote that night. By not destroying the letter and by never discussing the letter, Grace's father discredited it. The letter became an unanswered claim and portrayed again the liminal space of her transition and the power her abuser was not willing to relinquish.

While the letter was an important marker of Grace's empowerment and her movement away from her father's abuse, at the same time she was still under her father's control. Again, all transitions take place in liminal spaces where individuals improvise and move recursively and gradually. While physically Grace left her parents' home and escaped the abuse, she was still mentally and psychologically under their control. The transition appeared to have taken place and was marked by the letter, but she was still improvising and living within a space of both leaving and not leaving, of both escaping abuse and being controlled by her abuser. She described that after she left she felt both free and in danger: "I don't know. It was a relief, but I was still scared to death for my life. That was the thing. It was just like I was constantly moving for the first year because I was afraid." Despite her letter, the transition in Grace's mind was slower and more incremental. It took her a long time to find the courage to physically leave. After leaving, it took her months before she was no longer afraid. The internal transition took much longer than the outward appearance of physical movement or written statement of leaving seems to show. Grace described how she finally was able to overcome fear of her abuser and realize he could no longer hurt her, "It was probably eleven months before I seen him again, and then [after that] it was probably two years. Then, after that, it was—my adult pants got on, and I was like, 'Yeah. Screw it. I'm not afraid of you anymore.' Whatever. I was like, please say something to me, 'cause I will be a behemoth raptor all over you."

Grace was empowered through the act of writing the letter to her father. The nastiness and the putting down in words that she was leaving and that she wouldn't let him hurt her anymore became the impetus for the physical movement. She could have left that night without writing a letter to him, but the act of writing, or taking control of her own voice was an experience that stood out to her. While the internal transition took longer, Grace saw the act of letter writing as one that helped her take control of her transitioning, and she began to write other letters to her parents.

That first letter to her father became one of many to her mother and her father over the years. When recounting the letters, Grace never described them as healing, bringing solace or redemption. She felt compelled to tell her parents the hurt they had put her through. As Grace recounted writing these letters, it was clear the transitioning was still occurring as her anger overcame her. She described her mother as nothing to her, "the only thing she let me do is borrow her uterus . . . she was no mother."

Though Grace remembered writing lots of notes in school, folding them in complicated ways, and passing them secretly to friends, the content of these notes was not as memorable as was the act of surreptitiously passing them in class. Nor could Grace recall anything memorable she wrote for school. The most memorable piece of writing she described before her incarceration was the one that emancipated her from her abuser. This letter marked an important transition in Grace's life. It was a transition in which she took control of her own voice and safety.

DIANE: PAST STORIES IN FLAMES

Diane also discussed an important time of transition that she expressed through writing. This transition was fully internal and took place while she was incarcerated. Diane portrayed how the act of writing allowed her to recount and reclaim past traumas. She had not fully contemplated much of her past, but through writing, she was forced to stare down painful memories, and through this process, she was able to begin transitioning away from their control. Diane had a therapist in the prison who helped her begin the process, and then helped mark the space where Diane could visualize her transition.

> I wrote a lot. . . . I was really, really, really, really traumatized. I had a mental health worker come through and I wrote for her, to tell her—I was writing for myself, of course . . . I wrote [on] a yellow legal pad and I would just start writing. It's just like talking like this. One thing would lead to another, and a memory would bring out a memory. I wrote and I wrote and I wrote. I wrote for months, literally. *[pause]* Then we took it out and burned it.

Diane described watching her traumatic memories burn before her eyes as a critical moment in her healing. In her interview, Diane didn't share what she had written about, but she did describe that she was able to put a lot of painful experiences onto the pages.

My life up to that point had been just violence. I can't even describe and having all this stuff, just like a tornado in my head. Not being able to understand it, make sense of it, I think writing things out helped it not make sense, but be more real. [I realized] "I'm not imagining this." [My abuser] was so hell-bent on—my life was one big gaslight at that point, so the more I could write down, the more—the less sketchy it was to me. There were drugs and alcohol and just complete violence. The soberer I got and the more my brain started to bounce back, things got clearer and I could make sense that it wasn't—not so much make sense, but to just reassure myself that I wasn't the crazy one in the situation. His whole life had been dependent upon making me think that I was the crazy one.

Her memories were "sketchy" and she hadn't been "able to understand it, make sense of it" or even trust herself to see clearly what she had been through. The trauma and violence she withstood became clearer to her as she was able to write about what had happened. In her writing, she controlled the narrative. This control provided her with the power and space to transition. As she wrote down her memories, Diane entered a liminal space of sense-making and restorying. She made subtle, gradual shifts, and while writing she engaged in improvisation, moving toward and away from the narratives created for her by her trauma and her abuser. This transitioning through writing was assisted by her therapist who suggested that Diane write to work through her "sketchy" memories. Diane described the therapist as the impetus of this transitioning, and the experience as one that was similar to an outpouring of memories. "She [my therapist] was just wonderful—and it didn't have anything to do with the chronological order or anything like that. It was just this flood of memories, even from my childhood. It was just like this dump, but it took—oh, gosh—probably a month that I wrote." Diane described the day she and her therapist took the pages outside and set them on fire, and together watched them burn. She explained this as cathartic and cleansing. She was able to see that her past was over, and she could transition beyond it. At the same time Diane admitted that she wished she could have the experience again, "It makes me kinda sad, because I wanna do it again. Just in a different way, I guess from a different perspective . . . my perspective's gonna be different than what it was ten years ago."

The nonlinear nature of narrative transitioning is a part of Diane's understanding of this experience. The writing and burning was an important marker of an internal transition that was connected to healing, understanding, and moving away from the violence of her past. However, she had the desire to do it all again, knowing that while the process would likely still be healing, it would come from a "different perspective" in which her traumatic memories could still be addressed and described, but written after years of other experiences, and through a different lens.

Diane's experience of writing and then burning her traumatic memories marked her new ability to look at her past and unflinchingly declare what she had experienced. Writing out the memories allowed her to record the subtle movements and transitions. She could pick apart and slow down "the tornado in [her] head." Next, the burning marked her change within the liminal space of transitioning, showing her movement to self-understanding and healing. The writing was the impetus toward transitioning, and the burning created an erasure of the words and a symbolic letting go of past trauma. Certainly there was still healing that needed to occur, and Diane wasn't fully healed as she burned her memories, but the act of writing them down allowed her to visually comprehend the possibility of letting go and storying herself differently. She wishes she could do it again because the concreteness of the act allowed her to identify that she has transitioned and is transitioning, that her stories have changed her and she has changed the storying of her experiences.

BECKY: WRITING TO COMPREHEND OTHER PERSPECTIVES

Becky's story of transitioning, like Diane's, was an internal one through which she was able to use writing to view past experiences and see more clearly and from other perspectives. First she wrote a message to her daughter on Facebook. Second, she drafted a letter that was never sent to the DEA. Though the letter was never sent, her ability to imagine the response of a DEA officer led her to consider her responsibility for her past. Her transition was marked in a series of connected written communication with others, and her internal change came by considering the responses (real or imagined) of her audiences.

Becky lost custody of her two young daughters while she was incarcerated, and they were adopted into a new home. Becky was forbidden to contact them as children, but when they were adults, Becky described using the internet to find them and learn about who and where they were. Becky found her eldest daughter and began contacting her through Facebook private messaging. While they were not "friends" on Facebook, Becky's daughter did respond to her messages. When asked to describe an important memory of reading or writing following her incarceration, Becky described writing a particular Facebook message that brought about a change in her perception of a past event. She wrote a message to her daughter on the anniversary of her arrest; "I [told] her, 'Well, this is a hard day for me cuz eighteen years ago I lost you.' She [my daughter] says, 'Oh, I remember this day. . . I still have post-traumatic stress disorder.'" Becky said her daughter's response was unexpected and caused her to remember more about that day.

> [I remembered] the door blowing up, my front door blowing up. There's a grenade on the step frame . . . it blew up the door. They come running in.

> They're all in black suits. They got these gas masks on. They got guns out. [They were] raiding my house. I remember my daughters just got outta the shower. The little one, she had a towel around her. She was in the hallway. The laundry room doors blew off. They had [me] against the wall.

The original message that Becky wrote to her daughter was to acknowledge her sorrow of losing her children, not to relive the trauma of that night. The response from her daughter brought back the memories of that night and Becky was faced with the distress her daughters must have experienced. She hadn't faced her daughters' traumas in the past, and as she considered her daughters' points of view, Becky became furious about the effect of that night on her children and decided to write a letter of formal complaint to the Drug Enforcement Administration (DEA): "I went through that day and I'm like, oh you know what, I'm fixing to write them a letter. I'm fixing to write the DEA a letter and tell 'em what I think about what they did." As she composed the letter, her thinking changed, and she more clearly remembered that night through the description her daughter brought to mind. In the end, she never sent the letter because she began to consider her own culpability,

> By the time it comes to the end of the day I'm like, "But they were following their job. They were doing procedure" . . . because they don't know what they're going into. Whose fault was it? It wasn't their fault, it was mine. I had to take blame by the end of the day. It wasn't their fault. They don't know what situation they're going into. They're following procedure, this is how they do it.

What began as feelings of blame toward the DEA and protective anger on behalf of her daughter became a different sort of empathy for the officers involved. Though Becky didn't describe the situation the officers were "going into," her online conversation with her daughter, and then her drafting of the letter to the DEA allowed her to see the experience in a very different and more complex light. The message to her daughter began as a way to gain her daughter's sympathy and connection. The message was about Becky's own feelings; she explained the day was hard for her because it was the day she lost something. However, the act of reading her daughter's words on the screen—the words describing that day in her childhood memory—forced Becky to understand the event differently. When her daughter wrote that she was still suffering from PTSD from that night, Becky began to see that the memory wasn't just hard for her because she was arrested and lost her children, but it was injurious for her daughters, and the events of that night were still affecting them all these years later.

Becky described transitioning in her thinking about the events surrounding her arrest and her understanding of who was to blame. This liminal space of transition was marked as Becky began to see the night in question as a

layered event where she lost her daughters; where her daughters were traumatized; where officers were "following procedure" and possibly afraid for
their lives as well. Through writing to her daughter and then to the DEA,
Becky moved from seeing the night of her arrest as merely an event of
personal loss to an event in which she was at fault for trauma and fear and
loss. The event was no longer hers alone, but she saw it involved and affected
many people, both strangers and those she loved.

MEMORY, WRITING, LIMINALITY, AND CHOICE

These narratives of literacy experiences that describe transitioning also portray gaps and incomplete communication or memory. There are gaps in the
women's narratives and places where the stories seem to head in one direction and then quickly change course.

These narratives show the slow, invisible, and subtle movements participants went through in taking control of their pasts and futures, and how
writing and reading were tools in both the process and comprehension of the
transitioning. The liminal and nonlinear spaces of transition were marked
through reading and writing. Grace's letter seems to mark her break from her
family, yet she also describes it taking years before she felt she was safe and
could finally stop being afraid of her abuser. Even though she was no longer
living in his home, she was separated from him physically, but not emotionally or mentally. She was in the liminal space of being both free and controlled.

Diane's description of her memory of writing and then burning the pages
is also a marker of trying to comprehend and move beyond her past. She had
worked with a therapist to overcome some of the traumas she'd experienced.
The memories did not just get written onto the paper and then thrown away
to be forgotten. Instead, the words turned to flame and then ash as Diane
watched. It was a symbolic act to show that a transition had occurred, that
she was moving beyond her trauma. Even so, Diane said that she wished she
could go back and do the same again. Because the transitioning in her lived
experience didn't end with the burning of the paper. Here again is the nonlinear and liminal space of transition. While the burning of memories marked a
transition, it was but a visible marker of slow and subtle change that occurred
over many months of writing and therapy. Her transition did not erase the
memories as if she was moving in a linear process away from her past. The
narrative was recursive, and the memories were revisited from different perspectives as time passed and she transitioned further in her lived experiences,

Becky shared a story of how through reading and writing she restoried a
significant night that she found not only affected her, but also her daughter.
Becky recalled her daughter had just bathed and was in a towel, and there

were officers in black suits running into the house. But Becky does not describe where she was or how she felt when the explosion and raid occurred. Her only placement in the story is that they had her against the wall. She was a reporter of the story, but not an active character in it. The instance was traumatic; it needed to be reported, and Becky felt she could use her voice to speak back to the entity that traumatized her children. She could speak as a mother and as a concerned citizen through a letter she began writing to the DEA. When she decided not to send the letter, she finally began to see herself as an active character in the narrative. A character who held responsibility for the event and her daughters' trauma.

It is worth repeating that these women were never asked specifically to describe any changes or transitions in their lives, nor were they asked to describe writing about trauma. Instead, they were asked to describe memories of a time when they read or wrote something that stood out as important to them. The stories that were shared included memories of transition because literacy experiences can be important markers of the more slippery and complex process of transition. Reading what others have to say about an experience might help one understand memories from a new perspective, allowing a transition in perspective or feelings of responsibility. Writing down one's thoughts, whether to an audience or to oneself, helps to clarify one's own thinking, as the thoughts can be looked at, considered, and made real. Whether these words are on a screen or on paper, they provide both a momentum and observable visualization of change.

Chapter Three

"Because Our World Is Very Small"

Prison Libraries and Librarians

Within the realm of literacy studies, a number of researchers have written about incarcerated women's writing practices (Hinshaw and Jacobi 2015; Jacobi and Stanford 2014) and have provided evidence that especially for women, literacy skills and self-expression aid in identity formation (Curry and Jacobi 2017; Jacobi and Stanford 2014; Maher 2004; Sweeney 2010) and lower recidivism rates (Davis et al. 2013; Maher 2004; Willison and O'Brien 2017). Fewer studies have looked into the reading practices of incarcerated women, and those that do often focus upon formal programs—reading groups, college literature classes in prisons, and the like (Wiltse 2011). This chapter provides a close view of literacy practices and sponsorship of incarcerated women as related to prison libraries, an important but often underfunded portion of carceral education leading to more positive reentry experiences. While prisons are primarily destructive sponsors of literacy in this study (Brandt 1998) by withholding literacy materials and experiences and controlling expression, participants told stories of their prison libraries and librarians as constructive literacy sponsors which opened up not only new ideas, but new self-identities and opportunities for control and autonomy that were impossible in other areas of incarceration.

Justice-involved people suffer "information poverty," defined by Drabinski and Rabina as "a situation in which a person cannot access the necessary information to solve a problem or answer a question" (2015, 42). Britz further describes information poverty as a condition "in which individuals and communities, within a given context, do not have the requisite skills, abilities or material means to obtain efficient access to information, interpret it and apply it appropriately. It is further characterized by a lack of essential information and a poorly developed information infrastructure" (2004, 192). The use of the word *poverty* to describe the lack of information is an apt one, in that information within prisons and other constrained spaces is a valuable currency that can be used to free oneself in mind, if not in body. The access, interpretation, and application of information is also critical for incarcerated people who, when released, will need to positively reintegrate into society. Currently, prison libraries' only requirements are to hold legal resources for incarcerated people to use. This is an important foundation, but ultimately inadequate by satisfying only one fragment of the information poverty from which incarcerated people suffer.

Some prison libraries, such as those in New York, are modeled after the state's public libraries but may or may not be staffed by librarians. The materials available to incarcerated people beyond legal resources is inconsistent from state to state and prison to prison. Although studies have shown that education within prison reduces recidivism (Davis et al. 2013), many roadblocks keep books out of prisons. These roadblocks are often based upon fear of contraband hidden in the books themselves or within packages of books. Additionally, some prison administrators have created unofficial banned books lists based upon fear of what certain reading material may cause incarcerated people to think or do (Inklebarger 2018). Sweeney (2010) describes a long history of how reading has been used in the United States prison system as well as how books and reading material have been withheld as a form of further punishment for incarcerated people who do not comply with certain rules. Sweeney also points out that these ideas remain current as in the 2004 *Beard v. Banks* decision. The Supreme Court concluded that the restriction of reading materials was appropriate punishment to uncooperative incarcerated people (Sweeney 2010, 19–20).

Sweeney (2010) cited a number of states that had restricted books coming into their libraries, often for the reason that the books in their prisons had to be proven to be rehabilitative in some way (43). While this is a vague enough purpose in itself, Sweeney also shows how many of the titles that are regularly rejected are those written by or about African Americans (Sweeney 2010, 44), books such as *Paradise* by Toni Morrison, *I Know Why the Caged Bird Sings*, by Maya Angelou, and William Styron's *The Confessions of Nat Turner*. These books and others like them have been bestsellers, and critically acclaimed. Maya Angelou has even regularly been taught in US high school classrooms. The control of these titles shows the racism and fear that is woven through the prison system. These books focused on African American topics or written by African American authors are framed as dangerous by prison administration because the books which discuss issues of racism may stir up racial conflicts among the inmates and threaten prison security. More to the point, Sweeney maintains, "contemporary restrictions to prisoners' access to books seem to contribute to the maintenance of literacy as white property" (2010, 44). Books written by white authors and about the white experience, especially if those titles also present a rehabilitative theme, are therefore "safe" for inmates to engage with. This is one more way to exert control over incarcerated people.

Prison libraries and librarians were the most clear constructive sponsors of literacy for participants while they were incarcerated. Narratives of the prison library followed three themes: identity imagination and reformation; self-healing and self-development; and social connection. Identity imagination and reformation were often described through the reading of novels and short fiction. Through nonfiction books, the library holdings were also storied as sites for healing and self-development. Participants told stories of reading books about psychology, addiction, and recovery. Finally, the prison libraries were also storied as a space to connect or reconnect to the outside world. When libraries subscribed to local or out of town, smaller newspapers, at least two of the participants described using these newspapers as a way to see what was happening with their families and acquaintances back home. While participants' interactions with prison librarians were wide ranging, participants included detailed stories of prison librarians without prompting. This is especially poignant because the only interview question requesting stories about individuals was *What role models did you have to encourage reading and writing while incarcerated? Can you share any stories about them?* For all four participants, the prison librarian was the only human sponsor identified as residing within the prison walls.

TRASH INTO TREASURE: READING FOR IDENTITY REFORMATION

Escapism through reading was described often within participants' narratives, and it is to be expected that individuals whose bodies were imprisoned would search to free their minds through books. The books selected for escapism ranged across genres but were predominantly fiction. But while describing the books as spaces for escape, participants described these reading experiences as processes where they could reimagine and restory themselves. The novels allowed participants to try on the identity of powerful fictional characters. Diane told stories of reading novels and how even books not considered literary were important to redeveloping her identity:

> [I] just read a lot of classic novels while I was there. I read a lot of trash, too. A lot of escapism. . . . They had the most ridiculous series of trashy novels in that place. They had been passed around. . . . It was these strong, sexy women doing these strong things in these exotic places. It was just that. It was just pure escapism. It was a strong, assertive female character. It was empowering, and it sounds weird now and I just hadn't thought about it that way.

Diane described reading both "classic novels" and "trash." Though the trashy novels were "ridiculous" they also provided models of "assertive," "strong, sexy women" who were engaged in "strong things" that empowered her to see herself beyond the past identity that had been formed through years of abuse. While some politicians or educators might champion the reading of classic literature, here Diane shows that a novel lacking great literary merit still provides important models for women who have rarely felt independent or powerful. The exotic places and the plotlines of these novels, while illusory and outrageous, regularly included a female protagonist who had autonomy over herself and her surroundings, who could make her own decisions and prosper. The women who participated in this research study did not share stories of many strong, positive, real-life female role models, making these literary protagonists especially significant and unique illustrations.

Diane also described even the freedom to read what she wanted while she was incarcerated was something she had not experienced before. With access to the library, she was able to select her own books, resulting in a different view of her world:

> I know a lot of the ladies there had that experience, of being able to see things in a different way than what they had before. Just to have that freedom. I remember coming to the realization in there that I had more freedom there than I had before I went in. . . . With my ex-husband, yeah. With my life the way it was before. That was a stark realization as to the way I was living before, and how bad it really was. I blew through books in there, too . . . library was great. . . fabulous library. They had a full set of law books. They'd order books if you needed them. If you chose to take advantage of it, there was always something available.

Grace, on the other hand, did not describe reading a lot of fiction. Instead she told stories of reading many books in the *Chicken Soup for the Soul* series. She was drawn to these books because they included shorter pieces and positive themes. *Chicken Soup for the Soul* books are collections of positive, nonfiction, "feel good" stories, and these were helpful for Grace to stay optimistic and continue to see possibilities that were not readily apparent in her day-to-day life behind bars. Reading story after story of people doing good or situations working out for the better allowed Grace to view the world, and her place in it, through a more optimistic lens. She was able to imagine life beyond imprisonment with hope and possibility.

These participants' stories of reading showed books as beacons of hope to imagine other possibilities. The women were able to imagine themselves and the world differently. Participants' experiences echo research findings by Djikic et al. (2009) who found that individuals who read fiction became more empathetic, and the practice of fiction reading "lead[s] to a gradual change of oneself" (28), allowing readers to in fact imitate and envision themselves within other identities (Djikic and Oatley 2014). The connection between reading and self-identity was powerfully shown in Speer et al. (2009) who, through MRI imaging, found that individuals' brains were activated in ways that showed they were envisioning themselves in the character's place. For example, the part of the brain concerned with a hand clenching was activated when research participants read about a character clutching an object. The reading of fiction, for incarcerated women, provides a way to slowly and subtly try on other identities, preparing them for reentry and the work of creating a more positive self-identity, conceivably reducing the possibility of recidivism.

WINDOWS INTO THE SELF: HEALING AND SELF-DEVELOPMENT

Besides using books to imagine other possibilities and to reform identity, the women also described books as providing a new understanding of their own mental health and addiction challenges. Some estimates have indicated that up to 70 percent of women in prisons and jails have substance abuse issues (Mageehon 2008). Prisons are experienced contextually and women's past experiences, whether constructive or destructive, play a large part in how they negotiate their time, autonomy, and identity as prisoners (Mageehon 2008). Therefore, the stories of past substance abuse or addiction are carried into the prisons and continue to story and restory incarcerated women's understandings of power, control, and identity. Participants described prison libraries' self-help books as sponsorship that empowered them to redefine themselves and feel less isolated.

For example, Grace described the importance of a particular self-help book that she was introduced to while incarcerated: "What I read in the book would be I wasn't the only one. I wasn't the only one that had these issues, that other people feel this way, too, and it's okay, and you work through that." Grace described this book as an aid to her recovery program, and she explained that she read it until it was worn to the point of falling apart. This book was a significant, constructive sponsor, not only increasing her literate activities, but also providing insight into and new stories of who she was and who she could become. It sponsored the re-envisioning of her identity as a nonoffender, and a person whose experiences were not so different from many others. It gave her hope and a sense of independence and direction.

Besides this self-help book, Grace also depended upon a Bible organized specifically for those recovering from addiction. She held onto this Bible and turned to it throughout her incarceration: "I really got into a *Life Recovery Bible.* . . . They broke it down. Two-thirds of the page is the Bible, and then the bottom is the study. It just didn't deal with drug addiction. It dealt with all kinds of addiction—gambling, stealing, lying, cheating. You took that away from it." As she listed these addictions in her interview, she described the existence of thousands of other addicts in need of support. She realized through her reading that she was not alone, and her challenges were similar to many others. The *Life Recovery Bible* provided both a spiritual element and a logical understanding of mental health, two components that many twelve-step programs assert are integral to recovery.

While many prisons have addiction recovery programs available to incarcerated people, Grace described her interactions with these books as intimate, personal, and belonging solely to her. She told the story of how through a book she discovered perhaps the labels of criminal and addict weren't all that defined her. She read that many, many others could be labelled addict, but this label didn't fully define them, so it didn't have to fully define her either. Her story of this discovery included the unexpected insight that not only was addiction a common struggle, but also there are many types of addiction. Her discovery became her secret and her focus, and then her healing was something she instigated and controlled independently. This provided a purpose and autonomy during her incarceration that she selected and fashioned for herself, allowing her to transcend larger narratives that encircled her.

WINDOWS TO THE OUTSIDE: READING FOR CONNECTION

Besides literacy providing autonomy to women through identity formation and recovery, the resources in the prison libraries provided a way for participants to stay connected to the outside world. While isolation and depersonalization are primary punishments of incarceration, in conflict is the need for incarcerated people to eventually envision themselves as productive members of society. Within the walls of the prison, prisoners lose their identities and become invisible. They no longer have the familial or social context that provided their distinctive characters. Those within the walls, fellow incarcerated people and prison staff, do not know each other as part of any other social fabric. Identities become flat—existing only as "criminal" or "addict" or "victim." All forms of individual choice and expression are removed, and incarcerated people's stories from their pasts are inconsequential, erased, and remain untold. At the same time, stories of one's future are devoid of possibility, and current stories are swallowed up by the overarching and controlling narrative of imprisonment. If a justice-involved woman would like to hold onto any aspect of her identity from before incarceration, it is nearly impossible while cut off from communication to the outside individuals who may have known her as something beyond her identity as prisoner. This may be a positive experience for some women who needed to break away from a social pattern of addiction, abuse, or criminal behavior. However, for those who had support or caring relationships on the outside, the prison libraries were sometimes an important place where they were able to hold onto the positive identities from before incarceration.

Diane was one participant who described the importance of social connection through library subscriptions to small, local newspapers:

> We had newspapers from all over the state. We could go in and check on our people. It was a godsend. Then that's a terrible thing to—I mean because your world is very small. We would hear rumbles of things happening at home. People passing and things like that. Accidents or whatever. You can't get good information. We would wait and get our information in the newspaper. They'd have the *H__ News* or the ____ paper or whatever. We could keep up with what was going on. It was just a good thing. I think they [prison librarians] really did care about getting us good information.

Diane's comment that the "world is very small" reminds those of us on the outside just how small and solitary are the daily realities of incarcerated women. Especially for the many women who are isolated from children and other family members, receiving the news of those family members' daily lives allowed a sense of association to the outside world. The incarcerated women read about the schools, the events, the births, the deaths, and better imagined the lives of loved ones. Though the worlds of the incarcerated women were "very small," having access to newspapers reminded them of their contact with the larger world of which they once were a part, and to which they would return.

Some prisons rely upon prison employees to serve as librarians, to sort and check out books, but other prisons employ actual librarians to oversee the resources. Having trained librarians in the facility rather than a prison staff member provided participants with important literacy sponsors. This one type of sponsorship separated experiences in the library from the rest of the prison, and made incarcerated women feel like individuals, readers, and thinkers, all identities outside the stereotypical view of justice-involved women. Three of the four participants told stories of their prison librarians and described them in detail. Diane and Becky remembered their prison librarians by name, and shared stories about how the librarians helped them find particular resources. Diane said, "the librarian there . . . he was devoted to keeping us in quality books and periodicals, newspapers." Lexi, similarly, described her prison librarian: "he clearly cared about books, and clearly cared about you reading those books, so he would get them from other libraries, whatever library had the book you wanted. He was pretty good about making sure that you got to read what you needed."

The librarians were described as people who cared, who were "devoted," who not only found "quality" books but found the books an individual woman "wanted" or "needed." These women described the librarians as people who saw them as unique individuals with particular needs and tastes. The librarians were advocates for the women and worked on their behalf on the outside to get them materials that they needed or wanted. This was a source of human connection and constructive sponsorship that was significant in the participants' literacy lives.

Both periodical materials and prison librarians provided bridges to the outside for the participants. By reading about events in local newspapers, women could keep track of what was happening in their home communities. By working with a librarian who was not a regular prison employee, the women were seen and approached not only as inmates, but as individuals with particular reading needs and tastes. The librarians in particular were much more valuable than other volunteers or service workers. They were in fact central constructive literacy sponsors who indirectly assisted in the rehabilitation of the participants.

BOOKSHELVES TO SELVES

From these four women's stories there is a clear call for more robust correctional libraries and the employment of professional librarians. Not only is the very presence of these libraries important to women in order to escape the daily emotional stress of being imprisoned, it allows them to imagine themselves differently, as an individual whose identity transcends the label of prisoner. The libraries provide, for the incarcerated women, access to a new identity. She can see that there are stories about people like her, with addictions, who have been abused, who have made grave errors, and she is not alone in her experience. She can also see that there are other stories to be told and her story is still being written. She can discover other ways of life through novels and self-help books. Even what some may consider the "trashiest" novels could be resources of empowerment and identity transformation for some women. Such novels provide models of independent and powerful women, who took control of their experiences, and this opened up participants' imaginations to what could one day be different for them on the outside.

These libraries can provide an extension to one's "small world" of incarceration. Local newspapers can provide a connection to one's family, friends, and support systems on the outside. These allow incarcerated women to continue to imagine home and provide a sense of still being a part of that space though physically removed. Finally, when a prison library also has a professional librarian, volunteer or otherwise, women are able to connect with a human being who sees them as something beyond their crimes or the stereotypical stories society tells. The librarian sees the women as readers, as thinkers, as individuals with imaginations and curiosity that are unique and that transcend the criminal justice system. For an incarcerated woman to be treated in such a way by a librarian within the prison may instigate a change in how she begins to see herself.

Though federal and state prisons are required to have libraries, there are no further regulations except that they include legal resources. There are no regulations regarding the amount or type of other holdings. Besides the federal and state prisons, other corrections facilities have no regulations at all. Libraries with reach beyond the required legal resources in correctional facilities might seem excessive or unjustified, but based upon these women's experiences, the libraries offer more than empty entertainment for incarcerated people. They are resources for addiction recovery and sites of transformation. Through resources from self-help books, to spiritual tomes, to trashy fiction, they provide the first glimpse of possibility, empowerment, and freedoms that may not have been discernible before incarceration. While becoming invisible and disconnected from the rest of the world, resources such as newspapers and magazines provide a way to stay connected to those on the outside and allow an incarcerated person to see herself as a person who does belong somewhere, though temporarily detached. Finally, if we agree positive reentry and reduced recidivism are goals to strive for, the facilitation of extensive literacy experiences for educational purposes should be highly valued and increased. The multiple ways that prison libraries impact constructive identity reformation should be acknowledged as integral to goals of the correctional system. Here is an inexpensive and straightforward way to provide real change for people who are incarcerated that should be embraced and championed.

Chapter Four

Mothering through Literate Acts

Facebook, Texts, and "My Happiest Thing Ever"

James Gee (2000) theorized that while each person has a core identity which is a permanent "internal state" (99), we also have multiple identities that are enacted within particular contexts. Literacy is one of the ways in which an identity is either tried on or enacted, and this literacy-as-enacted-dentity is identified by Gee as "discourse identity" (100), or the enacted identity which is observed through written or oral communication. Justice-involved people are automatically assigned stigmatized social identities and are seen as depraved and dangerous criminals. Alternatively, current or formerly incarcerated women are often also assigned the identity of powerless victim. Prison becomes the place where these identities are reinforced and where they crystalize into an internal, permanent state, or what Gee would see as one's core identity.

Often, prison literacy programs strengthen criminal and victim identities through the assignments that are requested (Colvin 2015; Curry and Jacobi 2017; Hinshaw and Jacobi 2015; Muth et al. 2017). For example, incarcerated people may be prompted to write about their crimes within the framework that this exploration will allow them to be reformed. This sort of writing narrows their identity from the many other roles they may have had on the outside that complicate or contradict that of criminal or victim. An incarcerated woman's other identities—wife, friend, daughter, student, employee, mother—are flattened out or erased (Curry and Jacobi 2017; Hinshaw and Jacobi 2015; Muth et al. 2017). Colvin (2015) discusses the reductiveness of most narratives of corrections as black and white, us versus them, and focused upon narratives of punishment and redemption. Because of this reductiveness, she posits that many prisoners see themselves as having "untellable" stories if these contain both good and bad, or if they have experienced more than redemption, or if they demand treatment beyond punishment. When women are invited to write or speak of their identities without specific prompting, there is room for more complexity and true reformation as the discourse identities become more than just an example of enacting a transitory context-dependent identity. Speaking or writing without prompting allows freedom to enact one's more complex, multifaceted core.

While interviewed, the four women in this study were never asked to share stories about their crimes, nor were they asked specific questions about their personal lives. They were asked to describe important memories they had surrounding reading or writing. The interviews used chronological questioning that asked women to connect reading and writing to important parts of their lives, before, during, and after incarceration. It is significant, therefore, that when asked to discuss specific literacy practices, each woman, at different places in her interview, told literacy narratives that involved her children.

Opsal (2011) found that formerly incarcerated women regularly use narrative strategies to counteract the cultural identities placed upon them. The identity of "felon" was disrupted by their restorying of their identities in three main ways. First, they worked to contradict how society storied who a felon is. Second, they actively disconnected from their past stories of drug and alcohol abuse by focusing upon stories of their transformation. Finally, and especially important to this chapter, the women used motherhood as a culturally accepted identity to counter their identities as felons (Opsal 2011). The women in this study, like those in Opsal's work, shared stories about their reading and writing that sometimes also contradicted how society saw criminals. As they storied their identities as readers and writers, they provided counternarratives to the prescribed, negative criminal identities. These women layered culturally positive identities onto their stories and focused upon their identities as mothers, and the identity of motherhood is common to the population of incarcerated women.

In 2007, prisoners in the United States reported having 2.3 percent of the country's population of minors, or 1,706,600 children under eighteen (Glaze and Maruschak 2008). The act of mothering while incarcerated becomes wrought with contradictions. An incarcerated woman can see herself as a mother, which is a positive contradiction to her role as a felon (Arditti 2012; Opsal 2011). Yet, there are constant powerful emotions connected with the separation from her children. Guilt that someone else is mothering her children, or guilt from processing the harm that she may have done before she was incarcerated are both common (Arditti 2012) There is fear that the relationships with one's children will never be repaired (Arditti 2012). There is fear that children will be harmed while she is unable to care for them. There is a sense of loss that so much of the children's lives will be lived (Arditti

2012) without her witness. Lexi, Diane, Becky, and Grace described how they used writing and reading in their roles as mothers. Diane, Becky, and Grace described literacy experiences as positive attempts to heal relationships with children they had left behind. They used writing to help process who they were as mothers and to process the grief and guilt they felt while incarcerated. Lexi's experience was notably different from the other women as she described her daughters' advanced literacy as proof of her successful mothering.

LITERACY TO RECONNECT WITH CHILDREN

The prominent theme that occurred in the connection of literacy to mothering was that of using writing to reach out to one's children to reclaim or reconfigure relationships. The women in this study shared stories of letter writing and journal writing, which are what one might expect. However, they also shared more unexpected descriptions of digital reading and writing in which they connected to their children through social media or texting. Two women, Becky and Diane, shared stories that included reading Facebook messages and posts or exchanging texts; these acts of literacy allowed them to connect to their estranged children's lives.

Becky had been separated from her children for nine years while in a federal prison, and while she was incarcerated, her daughters (who were four and eight when she was first incarcerated) were placed in foster care, and later adopted. Becky, several years following her release, used Facebook to find her then adult daughters, and described her ability to connect with one through this medium. She explained that when she found her daughter, Adrianne, she was not ready to reach out at first. Because of the long time she had been separated from her daughters, Becky felt in some ways she didn't have a right to reach out to them. Becky lost custody of her daughters who had later been adopted by another family. Because of this, she was prohibited from contacting them while they were minors. Even when they were adults, Becky was reticent to contact them, and instead resorted to surveillance through Facebook and other social media. Becky told the story of reading a Facebook post in which her daughter, Adrianne, discussed her "birth mother," without the knowledge that Becky was in fact reading the post. Becky described reading this post as she spied on her daughter's social media following her incarceration. This story was the first narrative Becky described when she was asked to tell a story of something important she remembered reading following incarceration. Becky described reading the post that was about her: "It really broke my heart. . . . She still hated me, you know. . . . I went to her Facebook [page], we haven't friend-requested yet or anything. I read stuff and it said, 'don't even ask about my birth mother. I hate her.'"

When asked if she could describe how she felt while reading that post, Becky replied, "You know, I understand that." She then went on to explain how conflicted she was about reading her daughter's Facebook page and then later reaching out to her through Facebook: "My previous experience with drugs and the facility—I decided not to contact her—I said 'no, I'm not gonna disturb her life. I'm gonna see if she contacts me.' It's sixteen days from that day that I got a message on Facebook. It brought me to tears."

The message from Becky's daughter was to tell Becky about a memory her daughter had when she was in grade school. Following Becky's release from prison, she participated in a "stop the violence" program, through which she and other formerly incarcerated women went to elementary schools around the state, telling their stories to provide cautionary tales to the students. This program and others like it provide faces for the invisible persona of criminal, but they also reinforce identities of felon, criminal, victim; rarely if ever, is there space for participants to also identify themselves in positive ways or through identities that contradict society's accepted narratives of justice-involved people as criminal, as penitent, or as reformed. Through Facebook messaging, Becky's daughter Adrianne revealed that Becky had been at her own elementary school as a part of the program. Adrianne shared that she recognized Becky and it had been extremely painful for her to hear her share her stories. Becky summarized the Facebook message from Adrianne: "she said, 'I was in sixth grade when I saw you.' She says 'I was in the back of my class . . . trying not to hyperventilate.'" When asked to describe how she felt while reading that message, Becky said, "I knew [Adrianne] got adopted in [that city]. I always wondered. I always thought, 'she could be in this class. She could be here.' She was. She was there . . . it really broke my heart, cuz she was scared."

Through reading brief Facebook messages from her now adult daughter, Becky's identities collided. She saw herself as a mother who was finally able to reconnect with her daughter. She saw herself as a criminal who had traumatized her daughter. Through Adrianne's memory, she also saw herself as repentant and reformed, brought before schoolchildren as a victim or a morality lesson. But for her daughter, the lesson was not one of morality, but one of conflict and pain as she saw her mother on stage but was unable to connect her performance to an identity beyond reformed criminal.

After recounting this Facebook exchange, Becky described her current relationship with her daughter as limited to Facebook and only "a little bit. Not enough. She's not used to me." Becky named her daughter's adoptive mother during the course of her interview and explained matter-of-factly that since her daughter was raised by this other woman, she understood how Adrianne would see her instead of Becky as her mother. Even though legally the role of Adrianne's mother had been given to another, Becky still held onto her identity of mother, even if it was just through "a little bit" of communication through social media. She used reading and writing on Facebook to attempt connection with her adult daughter even though it meant she also faced conflicting realities of identities of mother and felon. Facing conflict and telling the stories of communicating with her daughter allowed Becky to enact a truer, more complex identity that included mothering, however limited that mothering may have been. She was able to see herself and story herself as a mother, something that is a culturally constructive role.

Like Becky, Diane also recounted important literacy experiences both during and following incarceration which were connected with her children. Diane, the mother of six children, reached out to her children through writing and had a more positive result than Becky. Diane's children were placed in the home of her mother-in-law while she was incarcerated. She described writing many letters to them while she was in prison, though she didn't know if her children received them because the children were not allowed to be in contact with her: "then after a year or two of writing and not getting any response it's hard to keep going. It was just very painful. I got lots of pictures, and I would get reports from other people that everything was okay. . . . I went for basically eight years . . . didn't have any contact with my kids." What pushed Diane to continue to write the letters was her love for her children, certainly, but also the stubborn determination to hold onto her identity of mother. Currently, she describes having strong relationships with all her children and regularly communicates with them in group texts and on Facebook. Though she describes responding occasionally, she mostly seems to be an onlooker, reading and enjoying her children as they speak to each other through texts. When asked to describe an important experience reading after incarceration, Diane joyfully described text messaging with three of her daughters: "We have this silly group text going on now, my three girls . . . my children are all so funny and so articulate and snarky and brazen and just absolutely hilarious. Those girls get going and they are so funny and so sharp. It's like getting your hair blown back. I can't even keep up . . . I don't know what to say [to them]. I send a smiley face back."

In further describing the importance of this writing and reading in her life, Diane portrayed written communication as a way to be closer at times when they have been physically or emotionally separated: "it's these texts, and it's the stuff on Facebook. . . . It's like a surrogate. It's the method, the means in which we have a relationship." Then she immediately discussed how she needed to prove herself to her kids and she was able to do this through writing, "I think it was just another means of me being able to prove to them that I do what I say I'm gonna do. This is really what I am. This is really who I am. It's been very valuable, I think, in helping . . . see that they can trust me again . . . I really wasn't sure . . . that I would ever have a meaningful relationship with any of my children."

For Diane, the reading and writing of text messages or on Facebook were almost voyeuristic. She was able to read with pride the interactions between her children through their group text. She could see how "articulate and snarky and brazen and just absolutely hilarious" her children were and find some joy and connection within those texts. Though her interaction was minimal—just a "smiley face"—she was still allowed into the communication. Her children identified her fully as their mother by allowing her to be a part of the group text, and she understood this as a gift.

GRACE'S INTERNAL DIALOGUE

While Diane and Becky used reading and writing to form connections with their children following incarceration, Grace wrote to maintain an internal connection with her children while incarcerated. Like the other women, she was unable to have contact with her children, so she kept a journal in which she wrote letters to them, envisioning what she would say if they were with her: "When I got to be with them again, I presented them this journal—and it was daily—How much I missed 'em, and I hoped that one day that they could forgive me for being gone, that I will be a better mother . . . they fought over it.—but the fight was on. It was on. 'I want to read it.' 'I want to read it.' 'It's my journal.' 'It's my journal.'" The journal was full of a mother's regrets and love, and writing in it allowed Grace to enact her voice and her identity as a mother.

She could portray her mothering even though she was unable to see or talk to or hear back from her children. Though writing in a journal, Grace was in an imagined dialogue with her children, and in this dialogue, she enacted her identity and was able to portray herself as someone who had influence beyond the prison walls. She had children she could speak with, ask forgiveness from, make promises to. The enactment became reinforced when she was able to present the journal to her children and she saw how they treasured and even fought over her words. Describing how her five children fought over the journal made Grace frustrated that they had to share something they found so valuable, but also pleased that they cared enough to want to read what she'd written. She hadn't been sure while incarcerated if they would have cared. In our interview, she said that she wished she could have kept five journals, so they wouldn't have to fight. When asked what she wrote in the journal, Grace described the following, "that I was sorry, and sorry I missed out on so much. I know what I'm missing. I don't want you to think that I don't know. How empty I felt there without them. . . It hurt. It hurts. It hurts. It still hurts today. . . . I cheated 'em."

While incarcerated, Grace's journal for her children became the place where she enacted her identity of mother and created an imaginary dialogue with her children. While her role was flawed in that she "missed out on so much" and "cheated 'em," she still enacted the voice of herself as a mother speaking to her children and sharing her hopes and her regrets. While incarcerated, the writing she did allowed her to self-identify as something other than inmate. Grace held tightly to her identity as mother, however painful, through these written conversations with her children.

SPONSORING HER DAUGHTERS' LITERACY: LEXI'S "HAPPIEST THING EVER"

Lexi's stories of literacy and mothering came from a somewhat different perspective. While Diane, Becky, and Grace shared stories of literacy experiences that were used to connect or reconnect with their children, Lexi's stories took for granted that her connection with her daughters was intact. Early in her interview, Lexi recounted her parents serving as constructive literacy sponsors, and described herself as a voracious reader from when she was young, "My mom read a lot before bedtime. My dad went to auctions when we were kids, so I would bring a book and read at auctions, to pass the time. I can remember in third grade, reading books, cuz we had an accelerated reader program. You would get points. I would read as many books as I could. I loved to read, honestly." However, when asked about her reading experiences following incarceration, Lexi did not describe her own reading. Instead, she focused upon her two daughters, and proudly described one daughter's reading ability: "my oldest daughter has picked up my reading, and she loves it, loves it. She's a third grader. She reads at a seventh-grade level. That's my happiest thing ever. I love to hear her read." That her daughter's reading is her "happiest thing ever" shows that Lexi's daughter's reading ability is a positive reflection upon her identity as a mother. Lexi, a self-proclaimed avid reader, likely had many reading experiences after incarceration, yet she chose to focus upon her daughter's reading. This description portrayed Lexi as both a mother and a constructive sponsor of literacy. Lexi enacted a mothering identity, which was successful and involved. She was not a mother isolated from and working to connect with her children. Lexi storied a strong, positive connection with both her daughters, describing her influence over their literacy skills. Lexi shared how her daughters' father worked to make sure the girls became readers despite Lexi's incarceration, "I was locked up when she was four. Her dad can't read that well, so he's made it really, really important to be able to make her read really well . . . [he] just read to her constantly—from the time she was little, all the same books his parents read, all the books we read. She can read well. I love it." Following incarceration, Lexi had a second daughter and she narrated the practice of taking both daughters to the public library,

> I still do [read to her]. Then I have a two-year-old, and we both read to her. . . . There's so many kids I've come across that can't read the way they should be able to. . . . What we've done this summer is found all the books by [a particular] author. She just goes and picks out her book . . . [we are reading] potty-training books right now [for the two-year-old] . . . no hitting, you have to share books. You read them, and then they just look at you . . . two is a hard age.

Lexi described her older daughter as reading beyond her grade level. This story was told with pride and framed her identity as any other mother who was proud of her child and taking responsibility for her school success. This was in great contrast to Lexi's identity as an inmate, and the expectation that her identity was defined as a victim or criminal. Through her mother identity, Lexi overcame the role of victim as she was instead in control of not only her life but also positively influenced the lives of her daughters. She contradicted the stereotype of a criminal because she was teaching her children to be better and more educated. Even though "two is a hard age," Lexi described persevering to bring her daughters up right. She used books to teach sharing, not hitting, and finding success in school. Lexi's stories were not of her worrying about her daughters in connection to her incarceration. Instead, the stories focused upon her present identity—an ordinary mother like any other, reading picture books to her daughters and taking them to the library to pick out books.

Becky, Diane, Grace, and Lexi enacted mothering through Gee's (2000) theory of discourse identity (100). Their motherhood was an enacted identity through reading and writing. This literacy-as-enacted-identity was sometimes reading the words of their children, as in Diane's reading of her children's group texts, or Becky's reading of her daughter's Facebook page. This reading provided a priceless window into their children's lives, and a window that identified them as mothers. Grace used writing to create a dialogue and a relationship with her children, helping her process the ways her identity as mother interacted and conflicted with her role as an inmate. Finally, Lexi fully embraced her role as mother to the point that it successfully swallowed up and erased her role as an inmate. Her daughters were readers, and her eldest daughter was reading at a level much higher than her peers. This provided proof that Lexi was a successful mother and this role weakened her incarceration as an identity marker.

Discourse identities are always identities enacted through literacy, and these women narrated their literacy experiences as connected with mothering, allowing them to replace the identity of ex-inmate with more positive and constructive ones. Lexi's narrative of constructive literacy sponsor for her children did not reference her incarceration in any way, except to mention that her partner read to her daughter every day while she was incarcerated. Then when she was released, she stepped in and continued the work of sponsoring her daughters' literacy.

The other three women, however, narrated their mothering in opposition to their incarceration. Their discourse identities were used to specifically combat the identity of justice-involved people through which they became separated from their children. By clutching onto and then imposing mothering identities through reading and writing with and to their children, they were able to reclaim their connections to their children while resolving the earlier pains of inmate identity. These identities were enacted through written communication directed to their children or participating in written dialogues with their children. Either way, the written dialogue empowered Becky, Diane, and Grace to have a voice within their children's lives and to hear their own maternal voices speaking loudly within their own narrative identities.

Chapter Five

The Three-Dimensional Landscapes of Formerly Incarcerated Women's Literacy Narratives

Patrick W. Berry (2018), in his study of literacy learning in a men's prison, emphasized that historically prison literacy has been tied closely to tropes of reintegration and hope. These tropes seem constructive but are actually problematic because they connect literacy directly and singly with successful reintegration and therefore erase impacts of social injustices and oppression. Further, these tropes establish educators who work with justice-involved people as saviors. While there are certainly connections between advanced education and better material realities for formerly incarcerated people, Berry urges educators working with justice-involved people to resist the pressure to depend entirely upon the argument that education lowers recidivism, especially in the case of literacy education,

> Rather than thinking of literacy and learning as something we do for some yet-to-be-seen purpose, I argue that writing and the sharing of writing are valuable in and of themselves. That is, reading and writing construct a *contextual now* that we can all inhabit. . . . I use the term *contextual now* to describe those acts of composing and becoming that lead to a deeper engagement with the world and one's place in it as well as to describe the value of being present. (14)

The narratives shared by Grace, Lexi, Becky, and Diane show how they have each used reading and writing to construct their own identities outside of those constructed by the criminal justice system. They were able to write and read in ways that led them "to a deeper engagement with the world." These literacy experiences also allowed them to interpret and create a world for themselves through the landscape of their stories. They have each shown what it looks like to create a contextual now and how these constructions have allowed them freedoms within oppressive and constricting landscapes.

As previously mentioned in chapter 1, narrative inquiry must consider a whole storied landscape to fully understand the context of a story. The three-dimensional narrative landscape identified by Clandinin and Connelly (2000) includes temporality, spatiality, and sociality, and provides a structure to not only examine narratives individually, but also consider groups of narratives as constellations of stories and storying (Craig 2007) amidst a sweeping and inclusive landscape. These constellations can provide insights into similarities and context that is not as apparent through individual narratives. In this chapter, I will explore the three dimensions of the narrative landscape as one may view it within a constellation of storying. These analyses will observe Diane, Grace, Lexi, and Becky's stories in relation to each other and through the lenses of temporality, spatiality and sociality.

TEMPORALITY

One of the three dimensions of a narrative landscape (Clandinin and Connelly 2000) identifies the ways stories move through and are situated in time. While all narratives are temporally defined, two of the stories in the previous chapters are especially interesting in the ways they use time to connect the narrator to her stories and identity over time. Lexi moves alternately back and forth through time to connect her own childhood reading experience to the reading experiences of her daughters. Becky moved back and forth through time as she narrated experiences of trying to reconnect with her daughter and finally coming to terms with her guilt in her daughter's trauma. Schaafsma and Vinz (2011) remind us that in narrative inquiry, the places where stories start are in many ways arbitrary. Though temporality in narrative can fluctuate and time often becomes fluid, narratives in research are always "in media res"—the literary term used to identify certain plot structures and translated from Latin to mean "in the midst of the action." Lexi's and Becky's narratives each begin from a prompt in our interview to describe a particular memory of reading or writing, but after their chosen beginnings, each woman's stories move dramatically and somewhat erratically through time.

When asked to describe times when she remembered reading before her incarceration, Lexi's response moved through time and topic. She first shared that she had been an avid reader and read while her father went to auctions. From that story, she jumped in time to the present and bragged about how her daughter is also an avid reader, connecting the narrative of her own childhood reading to her daughter's. Next she flashed back in time and described how her daughter's father read to their daughter every day while Lexi was in prison, and that is one reason why she is such a good reader. Finally, she jumped in time once more to the present time and described taking her two daughters to the library, and how the younger one at age two is being introduced to books and reading at a young age.

The temporality of this narrative back and forth through time shows how much Lexi's memories of reading are connected to her desires for her daughters and her role as their mother. Though she began describing her own childhood reading, this narrative quickly jumped to a comparison with her daughter and an explanation that her daughter's reading instruction was continuous, even though Lexi was incarcerated for several years. And today, she has continued to support both daughters' reading by taking them to the library. This movement shows how Lexi's narratives of reading and motherhood are intertwined and how her literacy sponsorship of her daughters has become central to her own understanding of personal literacy experiences.

Becky also moved back and forth through time during her narrative of contacting her daughter on the anniversary of her arrest. Becky began her story sharing a time when she had written to her daughter through Facebook, stating that it was the anniversary of the day "she was taken away." Becky recounted her message and then her daughter's response. This response then made her flash back to the night of the arrest and she described the chaos and the trauma that her daughter must have experienced. Becky's narrative then jumped back to the day of her Facebook message, as she described her anger and writing a letter of complaint to the Drug Enforcement Administration (DEA) on behalf of her daughter. She flashed back again, this time narrating from the point of view of the officers, and finally jumped back to the original date and explained she never sent the letter to the DEA.

Becky's narrative is a memory inside of a memory. It is a narrative that is told as a story of recognition and reframing of original memories. The temporality of this narrative shows how the story that Becky had lived by—that she should be sad that her daughter was taken away   became more complex as she was forced to see the narrative through the eyes of others, namely her daughter and the officers. The moving back to memories helped her see clearly that there were others involved in the narrative and this framing changed her narrative drastically from one of self-pity to one of responsibility.

The above two stories show narrative movements in time through flashbacks and movements forward. Both of these examples show how time can be used to reframe narratives and connect multiple narratives through and across time. Both Lexi and Becky's narratives remain unfinished and incomplete. Lexi will continue to mother and teach her daughters and raise them to have a love of reading. Becky will continue to rethink and reframe her experiences of losing her daughters and will likely continue to find ways to interact and become a part of one daughter's life even if it is on the outskirts through observations through social media.

SPATIALITY

Besides time, the space within which a narrative is played out is a second important dimension of all narrative landscapes. The narratives in this study, which focused upon prison libraries and librarians, were most strikingly centered upon the spatiality of the narrative landscape. Especially pertinent to spatiality as it is connected to power dynamics are Lefebvre and Nicholson-Smith's (1991) theoretical distinctions between dominated and appropriated space. Dominated space is the space that is "invariably the realization of the master's project" which is "usually closed, sterilized, emptied out" (Lefebvre and Nicholson-Smith 1991, 165). Appropriated space, on the other hand, is defined by the group, not the "master": "it may be said of a natural space modified in order to serve the needs and possibilities of a group that it has been appropriated by that group" (165). Therefore, prisons are by their nature dominated spaces, yet it seemed from the narratives in this study, the prison libraries became appropriated spaces within the dominated space.

> It is impossible to overemphasize either the mutual inheritance or the contra-dictoriness of these two aspects of space. Under its homogenous aspect, space abolishes distinctions and difference, among them that between inside and outside, which tends to be reduced to the undifferentiated state of the visible-readable realm. Simultaneously, this same space is fragmented and fractured, in accordance with the demands of the division of labor and the division of needs and functions . . . each spatial interval, is a vector of constraints and a bearer of norms and "values." (355–356)

Within the dominated space of a prison, prison libraries seem to help prisoners appropriate the space. While a dominated prison space overall "abolishes distinctions and difference," the appropriated space of the libraries provides a freedom for prisoners to live out distinctions as readers who have certain tastes in books or other materials. The librarians in these spaces brought with them a way to fracture the space by seeing the women not as homogenous members of the prison, but as unique individuals and as thinkers and readers. Certainly, the spatiality of these narratives contributed to the ways each contributed to the women's storying and identification as literate individuals, and not merely ex-inmates.

SOCIALITY

The final dimension of the narrative landscape is that of sociality. Relationships are often described in narrative research as a web of interconnected individuals across time and space. Clandinin and Connelly explain, "In narrative inquiry, people are looked at as embodiments of lived stories. Even when narrative inquirers study institutional narratives, such as stories of school, people are seen as composing lives that shape and are shaped by social and cultural narratives" (2000, 43). Certainly the four participants in this study are embodiments of their own lived stories, but the people they describe as being a part of their stories are also embodiments of the narrators' own lived stories. While these people are brought in as characters in the narrative, their relationships to the narrator as well as the narrator are key in understanding the complexities of the entire narrative landscape. Grace, Diane, Becky, and Lexi did not include a large number of relationships in their narratives. Even when the interview questions focused upon stories of individuals who influenced them as readers and writers, the women had fewer stories to share than at other points in the interviews. Parents and teachers were often mentioned; however, Grace was the only one who described her relationship with her father. The other main relationships described in the women's narratives included their children, their prison librarians, and a small assortment of various "helpers" that were constructive literacy sponsors, but who did not seem to be involved in lasting relationships with the women.

Grace's story of leaving home portrayed her father as a destructive sponsor of literacy. Through abuse, he affected her ability to learn and focus at school. In fact, Grace described teachers in her schools growing up who either approached her trying to help her with the abuse or whom she knew had approached the authorities reporting the abuse they saw as evident. As abuse does, Grace's abuser's power over her affected her learning and literacy development. While his abuse created trauma and overwhelming fear in Grace's life, Grace was able to find the strength to overcome his control and leave. The act of writing her goodbye letter was a story based upon one relationship and the transition away from that relationship having control over her present and future narratives.

As detailed in chapter 4, the relationships these women had with their children were integral in the way they storied their identities, observed their pasts, and looked toward their futures. Their relationships with their children proved that they had valuable identities as mothers, and they fit into a socially normalized role that identified them beyond their crimes or incarceration. Even Becky, who had very little contact with one daughter, and no contact with the other, told multiple stories of reading and writing that were connected to finding and communicating with her daughter online. The most important literacy acts that Becky narrated included trying to locate, learn about, and reconnect with her daughter. Here too, the relationship was a pinnacle of the narratives she held about her past and present and future self, her losses, her mistakes, and the possibility of change.

It is striking, though, that not many other relationships were included in these narratives. While literacy acts are often considered solitary activities, they are also activities of communication and many of the narratives in this study concerned women's communication through writing and reading. However, there was a very small number of relationships described within these narratives. Much of the women's reading and writing had to do with their children, or others who had in some way assisted them through a fleeting relationship.

SPONSORS AND COUNTERING AND CLARIFYING CRIMINAL NARRATIVES

The narratives of formerly incarcerated women in the United States are socially constructed around identities of the criminal, degenerate, or victim. Recent popular media such as *Orange Is the New Black* have in many ways further reinforced these narratives. These socially constructed narratives take power away from women when they leave prison and need more than anything the ability to control their own narratives. Society's definitions of the formerly incarcerated are not merely insignificant, fleeting perceptions; rather these have great impact on women's success and reintegration. A future employer may identify a formerly incarcerated person through the narrative of degenerate or untrustworthy and fail to hire her. The teacher of an incarcerated woman's child may identify her as a problematic mother because of the narrative that she is either immoral and evil or a victim and therefore an ineffective parent. This teacher would then be less likely to support the parenting or effectively communicate regarding the child's educational progress. There are many tangible collateral consequences stacked against women as they are released from prison, such as costs of reconnecting with children, and difficulties in finding employment and housing (Reiter 2017). The grand, socially constructed narratives are increasingly sinister when they become the narratives women begin to tell of themselves. The narratives become internalized and lived out, leading to recidivism and generational patterns of crime and poverty. It is crucial to identify and reinforce formerly incarcerated people's counternarratives as it is through these counternarratives that formerly incarcerated women not only exhibit but also seize power over present and future circumstances. Acts of self-definition in the face of destructive narratives flowing through and around one's body and heart are a rebellion of the most vital and revolutionary degree.

The narratives that emerged through Grace, Becky, Lexi, and Diane's interviews provide insight into experiences of literacy and the negotiation of a woman's justice-involved status. These narratives also uncover examples of how identity and transition can be negotiated, controlled, and marked through acts of reading and writing. Constructive literacy sponsorship of transitional periods, children, and prison libraries allowed these women to story their experiences in ways that provided access and positive identities. These sponsors also enabled women to provide counternarratives to the accepted socially constructed narratives that would deny entry into more productive spaces or growth. These sponsorships authorized Grace, Becky, Lexi, and Diane to narrate their worlds, allowing them to gain power over the oppressive narratives of incarceration. The women became more than their crimes through the stories they told. They were more than their past addictions or abuse or punishments. They were readers, writers, researchers, learners.

Through the transitions, Grace, Becky, and Diane used literacy as a tool to move through a period of time, to make sense of it, and to control its effect. By using writing to communicate, reflect, and otherwise make sense of painful times, these women put into words and controlled their narratives of movement and change. They transitioned by using acts of reading and writing and were simultaneously changed through these literacy acts.

As mothers, Grace, Becky, Lexi, and Diane all were sponsored by their children and by the role of motherhood. Through acts of writing to their children, or reading with their children, they were able to create counternarratives to the grand, socially constructed narratives of the formerly incarcerated. Lexi was able to portray herself as a superior mother through her narratives of her daughter's reading skills and academic success.

Finally, what might seem to be the most obvious of literacy sponsorship—prison libraries—provided more than just the expected access to knowledge through books. These libraries and librarians provided yet another promise of control for these women to narrate their own identities in positive ways. They were able to narrate their futures in hopeful ways where they would no longer suffer from abuse or addiction. They were able to create counternarratives showing identities as readers and learners while being held under the dominant narratives that they were nothing and could be nothing more than criminals or victims.

LOOKING AHEAD

In part II, many of these themes will be explored further through the extended study of Diane's experiences in college and her narrative portrayal of her transitions from incarcerated person to university student to graduate.

Diane continued to negotiate her identity through the act of reading and writing, and in fact claimed an identity within a counternarrative to the socially accepted narrative of what she should or could do upon release from prison, by becoming an English major. In part II, Diane further narrates her experience through identity claims as a student, especially a nontraditional student. She overcomes obstacles connected to her final decision of choosing a major field of study.

Part II also includes the narratives of three of Diane's college English professors. They share their memories of her as a writer and student, and while at times their narratives may conflict with the stories she tells of her experiences, they align in ways that show these professors to be constructive literacy sponsors. These professors story Diane in ways that provide her access and freedoms to overcome stigmas and further story herself as a student, a writer, and finally a college graduate.

Part II

Layered Narratives and Sponsorships: Diane's Prison to College Identities

Chapter Six

Listening to Diane

One Woman's Prison to School Pipeline

While part I of this book traced the narratives of four formerly incarcerated women and their literacy experiences, the second half of this book focuses on one participant and her unique experiences transitioning from incarcerated person to college student to college graduate. Diane participated in the original study covered in part I. It was clear that her success in higher education was unusual and further research was crucial to understand her unique experience. Therefore, part II of this book extends the research described in part I and focuses upon Diane's experiences as a college student.

EDUCATION FOR INCARCERATED PEOPLE

While approximately 40 percent of formerly incarcerated people return to prison within three years of release (Center 2011) there is a definitive body of research that shows prison education programs when done well drastically lower recidivism rates (Vacca 2004; Davis et al. 2013; Sokoloff and Schenck-Fontaine 2017). For example, Project Rebound, a program sponsored by San Francisco State University since its beginning in 1967, has become a model for other universities around the United States (Deruy 2016). Only 3 percent of the program's participants return to corrections, and more than 90 percent of the students graduate from college (Deruy 2016). These numbers are striking, but when compared to other California state statistics, they are even more remarkable. Over 50 percent of formerly incarcerated people in California return to prison, and San Francisco State University's overall graduation rate is also around 50 percent (Deruy 2016). The program's success is in part due to the holistic nature of support provided to students. Advisors help program participants with everything from housing to how to set up an email account (Deruy 2016).

There are other programs across the country such as the Bard Prison Initiative (BPI), which has expanded to thirteen other universities around the country, and Inside Out (Insideoutcenter.org) which brings traditional college students into the prisons to take classes with incarcerated people. Community colleges and four-year universities are experimenting with different program formats such as these and having positive results (Sokoloff and Schenck-Fontaine 2017). Especially innovative are those like the REACH program at the Community College of Philadelphia, which not only provide coursework to incarcerated people, but also assist formerly incarcerated people's transition to complete their degrees on campus and then pay for their on-campus tuition through Pell Grants (Sokoloff and Schenck-Fontaine 2017).

The aforementioned programs are uncommon however. Most incarcerated people do not have access to education while in prison, and when they do, mainly technical education classes are offered; very rarely do incarcerated people have the chance to participate in liberal arts education where they may have the chance to see themselves as scholars, thinkers, readers, and writers (Appleman 2019; Berry 2018; Sokoloff and Schenck-Fontaine 2017). Justice-involved people succeed when the education programming is more holistic and considers the humanity of the student. This sort of curriculum does not focus only upon vocational skills but considers the justice-involved student as a multifaceted being. Scholars have recently been advocating for the sort of programming offered by Project Rebound which considers issues and curriculum that go beyond skill-level concerns (Appleman 2019; Berry 2018; Novek 2017, 2019). For example, Eleanor Novek (2017, 2019) provides descriptions of curricula and pedagogy in a liberal arts education that focus upon issues of race and gender "because considerations of identity can transform incarcerated students' sense of self in the world and allow them to deepen their understanding of their own life experiences" (Novek 2019, 61). This is a hard sell, however, when funding is difficult to come by, and politically, many are still opposed to using tax money to educate incarcerated people.

Though the Pell Grant was eliminated for prisoners in 1994, prison education programs have still endured. In 2016, the Obama administration created a "Second Chance Pell" grant, a pilot program that partnered with select prisons and institutions of higher education. In June of 2019, Secretary of Education DeVos called to make the Second Chance Pell program permanent. Others have called for a lifting of the ban of Pell Grants in prisons, and many are hopeful that this may occur in the near future. Policy makers have seen carceral education programs as attractive in their proven ability to lower recidivism (Davis, Bozick, Steele, Saunders, and Miles 2013), assist reintegration into society and the workforce, and save the government money in costs associated with recidivism. Since men's prisons are larger and more numerous, most of the programs for carceral education have been connected to men's prisons, so there is less data available regarding how such programs affect women in particular (Brown and Bloom 2018, 2). Since it has been established that crime, incarceration, and reentry are gendered experiences (Arditti 2012; Bender 2018; Curry and Jacobi 2017; Ferraro and Moe 2003; Hinshaw and Jacobi 2015; Willison and O'Brien 2017), it is imperative to also look at the lived experiences and incarcerated and formerly incarcerated women as they negotiate educational programs and systems (Sokoloff and Schenck-Fontaine 2017). Brown and Bloom (2018) have identified that higher education provides contexts that allow and encourage justice-involved people to transform by increasing their cultural capital, providing a smoother path to reentry. However, few university faculty, staff, or administrators are even aware of, let alone trained in, how to support formerly incarcerated students on their campuses (Brown and Bloom 2018, 7).

Those working in the field of correctional education celebrate the promises of prison education programs that lower recidivism, but at the same time, they are careful to describe the complexities of creating education programming alongside or within incarceration and point out that the aim of education within these settings cannot be focused upon rehabilitation and making up for the problems of the prison industrial complex (Berry 2018; Erbe 2019; Ginsburg 2019; McQuaide 2019; Sweeney 2010). In fact, McQuaide (2019) describes her work as a writing professor within a prison as continually "moving back and forth between the *privilege industry* and the *punishment industry*" (102, italics in original). While a university, or educational initiatives in general, aim to move individuals toward privilege, the prison system is focused upon punishment and erasure. Novek (2019) even identifies the need for unique pedagogies as prison educators approach the paradoxical, "seeking to promote education—potentially a powerful tool of emancipation—in an institutional setting that is designed to obliterate personal freedom" (56). Within this system, women especially find themselves in further complicated educational constructs which follow narrow gendered assumptions of women's education and rehabilitation tied to caregiving and not necessarily to financial or psychological independence (Erbe 2019). Correctional education is full of inconsistencies and conflict, including the faulty assumption that a student in a prison education program could easily make the jump into a traditional college classroom following her incarceration.

Recent correctional education scholarship has broadened from education programs within prisons to more carefully consider an efficacious "prison to school pipeline" (Halkovic 2014; Halkovic and Greene 2015; McTier, Santa-Ramirez, and McGuire 2017). This prison to school pipeline corrects and reverses what scholars previously identified as the school to prison pipeline (Hietzig 2009; Wald and Losen 2003) as a pathway that propels urban, mostly minority children, through impoverished public schools and into the criminal justice system. Halkovic (2014) and Halkovic and Greene (2015) have provided studies on formerly incarcerated people's experiences in higher education and have identified that students who have been incarcerated bring unique "gifts" to campuses, allowing them to teach the university about how to deconstruct stigma, how to work within complex systems, and how one can be transformed. In addition, these studies assert that universities and colleges are responsible for providing support and advocacy while reducing stigma as a part of social justice missions of providing educational access to marginalized people.

DIANE'S UNIQUE COLLEGE EXPERIENCE

Diane's experience is significant because she successfully transitioned from incarceration, to being a university student, to earning a Bachelor's degree in under six years. She enrolled in college two years after her release and graduated four years later with a degree in English. Part II of this book focuses upon Diane's experiences, and is framed by the following three research questions. First, how does a formerly incarcerated woman narrate the transition from inmate to college student? Second, how does a formerly incarcerated woman's narratives of college identify sponsors of literacy and the power structures involved in those sponsorships? In addition to Diane's experiences as a student, it was also important to identify how she was storied by those who were teaching her, so the third research question was: how do college instructors narrate a formerly incarcerated woman in their classrooms and how do their narratives compare to the ways the college student narrates her own experience?

This study focuses upon Diane's narratives but also holds them in relationship with the narratives of her college professors to allow an understanding of a larger picture of the narrative realities of formerly incarcerated college students. This is to better comprehend the narrative landscape (Clandinin and Connelly 2000) of this unique experience, taking into consideration not only the chronology and spatial aspect of events, but also acknowledging the powerful ways that relationships impact narratives of lived experience.

Diane's Background

Diane was incarcerated for five years. While incarcerated, she was able to participate in a number of correctional education programs that allowed her certifications and job training. When she was released, she obtained a job working for the city doing landscaping work. She also had a supportive partner, Leo, who had earned a Juris Doctorate and owned his own business. Two years following her release, Diane lost her job because of funding issues, and she decided that it was a good time to go back to college as she had imagined doing throughout her incarceration. She looked into two schools that were in the geographic vicinity of her home. She finally decided on Eastwood University when she found out her daughter was attending the school because she liked the idea of attending college with her daughter. Diane described that she saw the "stars were aligned" at this time, and it just felt like the perfect opportunity to continue her education.

Originally, Diane planned to study within the social work or human services programs at Eastwood because she wanted to become an addictions counselor. Eventually though, she decided to change her major to English over time. She became close to a number of other English majors and faculty, and eventually served in several leadership roles. She was the poetry editor of the campus literary magazine and was inducted into the English Honor Society, Sigma Tau Delta. She described the whole experience as an English major positively except for the last semester during which she suffered new challenges and obstacles to her life and education. At the time of the study, she was working as an arborist, and she and her partner, Leo, owned their own tree trimming business.

METHODOLOGY

Through Diane's participation in the previous study, her experience was found to be a unique case which warranted further inquiry. Recruitment included a formal request for further interviews. Before the formal request, Diane had informally, through email conversations, shown to be open to further interviews. The study included three separate interviews focusing upon different themes of her transition from incarceration to university and beyond. She was also asked to share artifacts she had kept from college (notes, writing assignments, etc.) that portrayed her experiences while a university student. Diane participated in three interviews: the first two interviews were spaced two weeks apart, and the third interview took place two days following the second; therefore, all interviews took place within three weeks' time, and all interviews took place in a private office space near Diane's home. Each interview began with some basic warm-up questions to help Diane orient herself to the topic and her memories of the time period. The warm-up questions were followed by more in-depth questions that were designed to elicit narratives, memories, and descriptions. The first interview focused upon Diane's decision to go to college and her first steps making the transition, and it lasted twenty-five minutes; the second interview focused upon Diane's identity formation as a student and as a writer, and it lasted forty-three minutes; finally the third interview focused upon the end of Diane's time as a student and her degree completion and graduation, and this lasted forty-seven minutes. All interviews were audio-recorded and transcribed. Though Diane was asked to share artifacts from her time as a student, she did not choose to do so. She understood that her professors would be contacted for interviews and she identified the names of professors with whom she felt comfortable participating in the research. Several weeks following our interview, I emailed Diane with a few follow-up questions. She answered those about a month later, and those answers were integrated into the data analysis. Diane's interview questions were structured as follows.

Table 6.1.   Diane's Interview Protocol

Interview	Warm-up Questions	Main Questions
Interview #1 Decision to go to university and first steps	1. When did you attend college (start, end, how many years)? 2. Did you go to school full time or part time? 3. Were you consistently enrolled? 4. What degree(s) did you earn?	1. What were the things, people, events that you think helped you decide to go to college? 2. Can you describe any influences from your incarceration that affected your decision to attend college? 3. Can you describe any influences after your incarceration that affected your decision to attend college? 4. Can you describe any influences from before your incarceration that affected your decision to attend college? 5. Why did you choose the college you did? 6. Why did you choose your major? 7. Can you think of any other interesting memories about the time you were deciding to go to college? 8. Can you think of any other influencers?
Interview #2 Identity formation (as a student, as a writer)	1. What are the first things that come to your mind when you think of a college student? 2. What are the first things that come to mind when	1. What were the things, people, events that you think helped you see yourself as a college student? 2. At what point in time did you visualize yourself as a college

	you think of a college graduate? 3. Would you describe most of your friends as college students/graduates? 4. Would you describe most of your family as college students/graduates?	student? As a college graduate? What did that look like to you? 3. Can you describe any times when you felt especially prepared for college? 4. Can you describe any times when you felt especially unprepared for college? 5. Can you describe any individuals at the college that affected your ability to see yourself as a student? 6. For part of this case study, in order to get a more rounded view of who you were as a student, I would like to interview some of your former professors. Are there any that you would like me to interview? Do these professors know that you were incarcerated at one time? Would you prefer I do not share that with them if they do not know?
Interview #3 Degree completion	1. How does it feel to be a college graduate? 2. What did going to college do for you? 3. Only 30 percent of the population the United States holds a Bachelor's degree, and fewer people who were formerly incarcerated. What do you think makes you different from most?	1. What were the things, people, events that you think helped you complete college? 2. Were there ever times when you thought you wouldn't complete your degree? What made you continue? 3. When you look back on your time as a student, are there memories that you are proud of? 4. When you look back on your time as a student, are there things you wish you'd done differently? 5. How did it feel when you were finished? Can you describe when you felt you had finished?

Within the context of the previous study, Diane stated she had revealed her correctional experience to several of her professors, so it was likely they would have previously considered her transition from incarceration to college. Diane identified four professors within the English department at Eastwood University whom she gave permission to interview about her experi-

ences as a student. The four were contacted by email and a basic explanation
of the study was provided, though Diane's identity was not revealed. If
interested in learning more about the study, the professors were invited to
sign an attached confidentiality statement. Before revealing sensitive information regarding the study (subject's name, informed consent, etc.) the faculty participant signed a statement confirming to keep the subject's identity
confidential as she was promised anonymity as a participant in the study.
Three of the professors signed the confidentiality forms and returned them.
One professor never responded. The three professors were contacted by
phone and the details of the study, including their role and Diane's identity,
were revealed. Each of the three professors expressed that they did remember
Diane from their classes, and they agreed to be interviewed. Following the
phone calls, professors were emailed a letter of informed consent and a list of
interview questions. The interview protocol was designed to be asked in
three stages. The first stage was made of warm-up questions and included
mainly logistical information. The second stage was designed to elicit participants' narratives of Diane as a college student. The third stage was designed
to complicate or clarify the previous narratives by including Diane's identity
as a formerly incarcerated woman. Interview times and locations were sched-
uled through email, and participants were able to select a location of their
interview that would be most comfortable and convenient for their schedules.
One professor, Justine, was interviewed in a private office space on her
campus. Max elected to be interviewed in his home, and Kevin was interviewed in the home of the researcher. The interview questions used with each
professor follow.

Table 6.2.   Diane's Professors' Interview Protocol

Interview Section	Questions
Warm-up Logistic Information	1. Do you remember what class you had Diane in as a student? 2. What is the focus of that class? 3. Can you describe the class in general? For example, what are some of the things you do in that class (activities, topics, assignments) when you teach it? 4. Do you remember meeting Diane in your class? Or do you remember when you became aware of her as a student?
Part 1 Narratives of Diane as a Student	1. What sort of a student was Diane during class periods? Can you describe how she participated or how she interacted with you or other students? 2. Can you describe any interactions you had with her outside of class? Did she come to office hours, meet with

you after class, schedule conferences? Other interactions?

3. Can you describe the kind of work she did in your class?
4. How did she compare to other students you have worked with?
5. Are you familiar with other activities or work she did on campus?
6. Do you have any other memories of Diane or the work she did in your class.

Part 2
Narratives of
Diane as a
Former Inmate

1. Did you know when you worked with Diane that she was formerly incarcerated?
2. When and how did you become aware that Diane was formerly incarcerated?
3. Did that information change the way you saw her or the way you worked with her?
4. Do you think other faculty or students knew this, and why do you think so?
5. Is there any other information you would like to share with me regarding your interaction with Diane when she was a student?

All professors' names are pseudonyms. Interviews were audio-recorded and transcribed and were all approximately forty minutes. Following the interview, Kevin also emailed scanned copies of his evaluative responses to Diane's writing. These included responses to six different writing assignments and two writing portfolios but not the assignments themselves. This data provided exceptional information as it portrayed his perceptions of Diane's work in the moment that she was his creative writing student.

Participants

While the main participant and focus of the study is Diane, the three additional participants were interviewed to portray how Diane was perceived as a college student. Justine was a literature professor and was Diane's instructor as well as her advisor. Max also was a literature professor who taught Diane in his literary theory class. Kevin was a creative writing professor who had Diane in several classes and was also the faculty sponsor for the literary magazine for which Diane was an editor.

Interviews with both Diane and her professors were fairly informal and though researchers must always be aware of the power dynamics between themselves and the participants, the interviews were conversational and relaxed. This is likely because Diane and I had already established a relationship from the first part of the study, and we had already talked about the possibility of an extension of that study. She was enthusiastic about sharing her story and comprehended the purpose and motivation behind the research in a way she may not have while interviewed for the first part of the study. Interviews with the professors were also fairly relaxed. Because these three were professors, they were my peers, and understood why I was performing such a research project. I had also been in contact with each several times by email and by phone to discuss the project before the formal interviews. They each had fond memories of Diane and were enthusiastic about sharing their memories. There was a small bit of trepidation among the professors that they were not providing enough information "to help" me, or that their memories were too fuzzy, but they were overall earnest and forthcoming in their answers to interview questions.

ANALYSIS

It was imperative during the analysis that Diane's experience took precedence and that her data centered the research, so the coding of her transcripts was completed first and without influence by the professors' input. As a narrative inquiry, Diane's stories were those most central to this study. Her interpretation of her own lived experience and how her narrative landscape affected the ways she identified herself, her past, and her future were the primary purpose of this study. It was also important to identify how Diane's narratives were either in correspondence with some of the larger social narratives such as those of college completion and degree selection processes; traditional college student identity; and correctional education identity expectations. Since professors' roles are often part of the power structures that promote and reinforce these social narratives, it was important that Justine, Max, and Kevin's perceptions of Diane and their stories of Diane were kept separate from her own personal narratives to ensure an authentic portrayal of her lived experience. This is also why their stories have been illustrated and analyzed within a separate chapter (see chapter 9).

Since Diane selected particular professors to be interviewed, it is likely that she selected the professors with whom she had strong relationships, those with whom she had positive interactions, and those who had influenced her. Because the professors were selected by Diane, and because they were all members of the English department, their transcripts and other data were viewed through the framework of literacy sponsorship (Brandt 1998). They likely were the professors who provided some sponsorship for Diane while she was a student. The data was coded to identify themes of how the professors perceived Diane as a student, and also how they enacted their own roles as sponsors of literacy for Diane.

As mentioned in the first chapter of this book, narrative inquiry is a layered approach to research which considers a three-dimensional narrative landscape. The three dimensions are: the temporal (how the narrative and

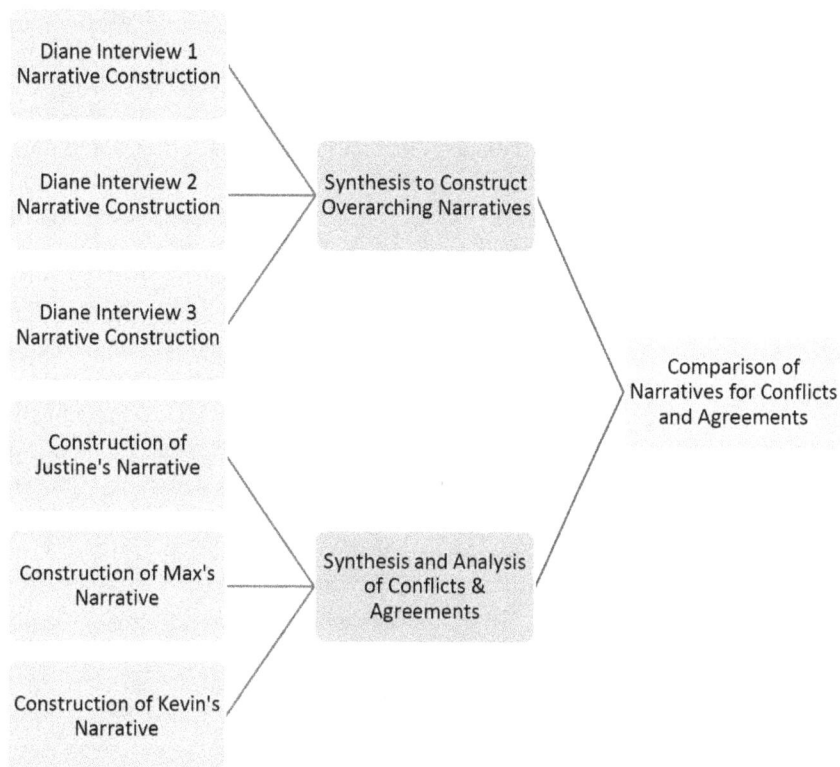

Figure 6.1. Phases of Analysis. *Graphic created by author*

narrator exist in time), the relational (how narratives exist among and affect human relationships), and the spatial (how narratives exist within space and context) (Clandinin and Connelly 2000). As a narrative inquirer, I was aware of these three dimensions as well as how I personally fit into the narrative landscape. As soon as I interacted with Diane and the other participants, I became a part of the relational dimension of the landscape. I was an audience requesting stories that may have been previously told or kept secret. I requested stories that may have been previously unconscious, personal tellings. These may have been to the participants, stories to live by but not to announce to others. Or, they may have been common tellings, stories that had been shared amongst family members, colleagues, or friends; they may have been stories that participants had already configured into writing or vocalizations, and the narrations shared with me were merely retellings of common narratives that had been cemented into the narrators' landscapes. Because of this, I acknowledge that my requesting narratives and then my constructing of narratives is dependent upon my own narration of the topics at hand and of my own experience. To better uncover the layers of narration, there were multiple research texts: interview transcripts, emails, and classroom artifacts. There were multiple participants. Finally, there was a carefully designed, layered process to analyze the research texts.

First the transcripts from Diane's three interviews were coded and analyzed three separate times. The first phase of coding was a descriptive and holistic reading of each of Diane's three interview transcripts. At the end of this first reading, I wrote a summary and reflective statement to identify the narratives included in each separate interview. I also went back to Diane's emails to me and observed any additional details that could influence the summaries or my reflection of her experiences. The second phase of coding included sets of thematic codes identifying constructive and destructive categories influencing Diane's college identity and experiences. I inductively identified these themes from the first phase of coding the data. There was a total of nineteen codes; one was for logistical information that may influence other themes and findings. Ten codes applied to narratives of constructive influences and eight codes applied to narratives of destructive influences. While these influences included narratives of literacy sponsorship, they also included broader and more abstract influencers such as "timing" or "finances."

The second stage of analysis focused upon only the professors' transcripts and artifacts. For each professor, transcripts were first coded holistically, looking for general themes and repetitive descriptions. Next, narratives were created for each professor separately. Finally, themes and narratives were compared to identify shared or contradictory narratives amongst the professors.

Finally, in the third stage of analysis, the two earlier stages were analyzed in conversation with each other. In other words, I reevaluated the codes and compared narratives to identify areas where stories were reinforced across participants and where they were inconsistent or incompatible.

The multiple levels of data collection and analysis were carefully designed and carried out to create layers of narrative understandings of Diane's experience through her own perceptions and the perceptions of her professors. As more justice-involved people enroll in higher education, it is important to portray their experiences as not only contingent upon their own narrative understandings, but also the narrative understandings of a politically charged context where there are varying power dynamics and both constructive and destructive narratives which control access to educational success. Since scholars have shown that certain groups of college students, in particular first generation (Soria and Stebleton 2012; Swecker, Fifolt, and Searby 2013) and nontraditional (Gilardi and Guglielmetti 2011; Panacci 2015), hold lower levels of social capital and have had fewer constructive literacy sponsors, it is important that any qualitative study of a formerly incarcerated woman's lived experience in higher education include the insights of those who have the power to provide or withhold the social capital needed to succeed in college.

With these complexities and power dynamics in mind, the study's findings provide a unique and significant portrait of one student's narration of her college experiences. The narrative analysis of Diane's experience is detailed in the next four chapters of part II.

OVERVIEW OF PART II

Chapter 7 includes the discussion of Diane's success as she began college. To begin, Diane's story was unique in that she had the financial and psychological support that many justice-involved women lack. Beyond this very powerful support, Diane was unique in that she had a secure narrative of her identity as a learner from a very young age. This narrative continued from her childhood and into her incarceration as she successfully participated in multiple prison education programs. Finally, Diane had a powerful model of a particular nontraditional college student who helped her narrate her own ability to attend college even though she wasn't a traditional, straight from high school college student. Many of the narratives Diane told were directly conflicting with the overarching cultural narratives of who a formerly incarcerated woman is and who a college student should be.

Chapter 8 analyzes narratives of Diane's experiences during college and beyond. As a university student, Diane changed majors and was able to redefine her purpose for attaining her degree. Much of her narrative portrayed the great sense of inclusion and support she felt as an English major in Eastwood University. At the same time, Diane told the story of problematic advising that set her back and complicated her degree completion. She also shared a story of personal trauma that occurred during her last semester as a college student. While overall Diane's narrative of her experience as a college student was positive, her story includes advising setbacks that are unfortunately too common, and stories of trauma that are woven within too many women's narratives whether or not they are seeking a college degree.

Chapter 9 provides an analysis of three of Diane's professors' narratives. These three professors, Justine, Max, and Kevin, provide their own narratives of how they saw Diane as a student, and particularly as a major within their department. This chapter shows where Diane's narrative of her college experience overlaps and contradicts with the narratives of her professors. It also shows where different professors may narrate the same student in different ways.

Finally, chapter 10 provides an overview of findings, provides suggestions for future research, and proposes implications that come from Diane's storying of her university experience.

Chapter Seven

Narrating and Owning a College Student Identity

As previously discussed, formerly incarcerated women face great setbacks upon their release, many of which are specific to their gender. Release means the return to families where they may or may not find support. If supported, they must still rebuild relationships with children and partners. Others, who had toxic relationships with partners or others, following release find themselves suddenly alone, perhaps also as a single parent. These women are often saddled with debt and other financial responsibilities while searching for employment. Therefore, for most justice-involved people, college seems beyond their reach, or in most cases, not something that could even be a priority when a job, a place to live, and custody of one's children must all be obtained. It is challenging enough to successfully transition to a life outside of prison without complicating it with the thought of transitioning to college, even if one was involved in a correctional education program while incarcerated. While a college education would greatly improve a formerly incarcerated person's likelihood of successful reentry and lower her likelihood of recidivism, attending college for many is an unrealistic goal. If a woman who has been incarcerated attempts to earn a college degree, the probability of her completing a degree within six years is extremely low.

Even without the traumatic experiences of incarceration and the stigma incarcerated women face upon their release, many colleges are struggling to improve completion rates for their traditional student population. A recent study of the general population of students who began their freshman year of college in 2011 showed that just under 57 percent completed a degree within six years (Shapiro et al. 2017). Students who were older had a lower completion rate. Only 41.7 percent of nontraditionally aged students completed a degree in six years, while 61.7 percent of traditionally aged, direct from high school students completed degrees (Shapiro et al. 2017). Students who delay college until they are older often have more responsibilities that may interfere with their studies. They are also less likely to be actively engaged in campus life. This engagement has been shown to be a predictor of college persistence and completion (Goncalves and Trunk 2014; Kahu and Nelson 2018).

First generation college students have been identified as particularly sensitive to lower completion rates (Soria and Stebleton 2012; Swecker 2013). First generation college students are less likely to be engaged in campus activities and resources, and they also report lower classroom engagement (Soria and Stebleton 2012). They often feel isolated and lack the social capital that other students naturally bring with them to campus. Since most formerly incarcerated people who decide to pursue a college education are first generation college students, they come to campus already lacking social capital. On top of that, they are of a nontraditional age, and often are confronting intense financial, mental, and psychological obstacles that naturally accompany reentry into society. Statistically speaking, this group should not be able to complete a college degree even if they do have the financial and mental support to first enroll in college classes. Diane's story is a unique case because of the opportunities and cultural capital she experienced that are unusual for most justice-involved women. First of all, she is white, which provided her immense cultural capital, especially on a college campus. She had a family that supported her pursuing a degree. She also had the financial support of her husband and social capital that came from her experiences as a student before and during incarceration. Even with all these advantages, Diane faced challenges, and if she'd had fewer advantages, the same challenges likely would have caused her to abandon her studies.

Diane attended Eastwood University full time from 2010 to 2014, and she earned a bachelor's degree in English with an emphasis in creative writing. She had been to college before her incarceration; in 1985 she attended a community college for two years in another midwestern state. Diane had been released for two years before enrolling in classes at Eastwood University. When asked why she decided to attend at that time, she described it just being the right time, "I just felt it. All the stars aligned. I was in a . . . very secure, stable relationship and just—everything was just right. We could afford it. I had some assistance. My family life was stable. [My workplace] went through a downsizing period and I lost my position . . . it was perfect." Part of the perfection of the moment was in fact that she had lost her job, so it made sense to go back to school. A college degree would make her more employable, and obtaining one was a goal she had held for years. Diane's partner, Leo, was extremely supportive of her going to college; he had an advanced degree and was financially able to support Diane as she earned her degree. Diane described Leo's support of her studies:

He has multiple degrees. He has a degree in criminal justice and then a JD and practiced law for a number of years. He was smart and encouraged me to just do whatever I wanted to do and I guess that at that time, it was just obvious to me that if there was anything that I wanted to do to better myself, that he would always encourage me and support me in that. He wanted me to do what I wanted to do and that's what I wanted to do, so we made it happen.

Diane was in a unique position since her partner had experience in higher education, and he valued higher education. Leo encouraged her to pursue her degree and was able to support her financially. She attended college full time without worrying about the cost or having to work while she was a student. This financial and psychological support made a critical difference in her electing to attend college as well as her ability to complete her degree. Few formerly incarcerated women are able to step into such a support system following their release.

Scholars in criminal justice describe the process of reentry as much more complicated than previously envisioned. Alexander (2012) explains that those who are released from prison are not released into regular society. Rather, they are released into a social "undercaste" (187) in which they no longer have the basic rights of citizenship. Reiter describes this undercaste as one based upon collateral consequences that are distinct from criminal punishments (2017) and identifies that formerly incarcerated people suffer a "civil death" even though they have been released. Laws limiting incarcerated people's civil rights have increased since the 1980s and include voting rights, access to public benefits, and immigration consequences (Alexander 2012; Reiter 2017). As recently as the 1960s there were laws that automatically ended marriages when one was convicted of a criminal offense (Reiter 2017, 63). The 1997 Adoption and Safe Families Act terminated parental rights to children who have been in foster care for fifteen of the prior twenty-two months (Reiter 2017). If a woman is incarcerated for just a little over a year, she can lose her children to adoption. If a woman is incarcerated for less than a year, she must, upon release, work to prove she has a stable income and home situation in order to move her children out of the foster system before the fifteen-month deadline causes her to lose parental rights permanently. As we are entering our fourth decade of mass incarceration, there are now 44,500 different collateral consequence laws across the country (Reiter 2017, 67). These affect all people who were formerly incarcerated, but these collateral consequences are a gendered issue because they are now radically affecting the children of these individuals and whole communities where women are no longer allowed to mother their own children. Further, many women are overwhelmed upon reentry with the myriad and tangle of collateral consequences they must negotiate. These are often deeply emotional as well as mentally and intellectually confounding and can easily cause justice-involved people to lose hope of successful reintegration.

DEVELOPING A POSITIVE IDENTITY AS A NONTRADITIONAL STUDENT

It was clear that Diane saw herself as a college student and narrated her identity in a way that conflicted with the accepted cultural narrative. She had previously been a college student (though unsuccessful), and she was white. Both of these provided her with advantages over most formerly incarcerated women. She had some experience with the culture of a college campus, and her race automatically provided her with a privilege that students of color do not have. When asked what comes to her mind when thinking of a college student, Diane's first reaction was to reiterate the socially accepted definition of a traditional college student, "Oh gosh. An eighteen-year-old. Yeah, just a much younger person . . . like my son, and my daughters, and their friends." However, she later began to describe a memory of a classmate she'd known who was quite the opposite of that description:

> When I was first—I went to college back in 1985 . . . there was a woman there who was in her late 80s, mid-80s. Her name was Margaret Stone. She was just wanting to go to school. She was there and got her degree while I was there. I had her in some classes. You'd see her around campus. I just thought that was *[gasping]* the most amazing thing. She did have a purpose, but she wasn't in it for a job or anything. She was there to learn. I just thought that was the most amazing thing. [She was] wonderful. Just a smart, sharp, sarcastic woman. She was part Native American, so she had stories and a wealth of experience to share with people. Yeah, it was such a great experience.

So, though Diane's first reaction was that college students were "much younger" and like her children and their friends, she expressed in much more detail and in a more emotional way the description of an eighty-year-old woman who was her classmate at the community college before incarceration. Though the common narrative of who college students are was a part of her understanding, Diane also personally identified with the more powerful counternarrative of an older, experienced, and inspirational role model. This narrative countered the cultural narrative of a traditional college student while undergirding her own identity as a college student. The traditional college student is one who is direct from high school, living on campus and with few, if any, other personal and family responsibilities. A traditional college student is also expected to identify a major as if they were selecting a job training program, with an interest in how a particular college degree will move them into a particular career. Diane's narrative of a college student identity included the "young," direct-from-high school aspect, and she also began her college career with a particular career goal in mind. She began college hoping to become an addictions counselor, but as she continued her coursework, she began to see herself fitting more into the conflicting narrative that she held of Margaret Stone.

Margaret, her eighty-year-old former classmate, was "smart, sharp, sarcastic" and had "a wealth of experience to share." Diane described how Margaret's age, rather than setting her apart, was a benefit to her college studies. She was also in college just to learn and Diane saw that as "the most amazing thing." These specific descriptors are much more detailed than Diane's first response, "a much younger person," which was more in line with the accepted cultural narrative, and these descriptors reinforced Diane's own identity. She was also older and also had stories and experiences to share in her classes. Eventually, as Diane changed her major from human services to creative writing, she again was able to look to the narrative she held of Margaret and how she was "there just to learn." Diane in fact echoed this narrative as she described her own experience of why she was in college, "I said this before. I didn't really come so much for a piece of paper as I did to learn and to make connections and learn about myself and what I was capable of." Diane's success in college was due in part to her ability to restory the accepted narrative of a college student's identity and purpose. Luckily, she had an example in a former classmate to help her create and see herself within this contradicting narrative.

DEVELOPMENT OF STUDENT IDENTITY WHILE INCARCERATED

Diane also described envisioning herself as a student while she was incarcerated, and some of the ways she described herself as a student directly echoed her description of Margaret:

> I guess I've always had the same vision of myself, even when I was [incarcerated]. I know that I'm older than the general college population. I came into school with a lot of experiences and some education that I think—I think some people think that being older when you go back to school is a detriment, but I absolutely do not believe that. I think the older you are, the better idea you're gonna have what you wanna do and you can be an asset to your professors and the other people in your classroom, just by virtue of that experience. Yeah. I've just always loved the academic setting and I love to learn and I'm a—just read voraciously and that always was there, no matter what my life was looking like at the particular time.

Margaret was experienced and was in college not for particular job training but just to learn. Diane described herself in similar ways. Though Diane was in her fifties, she also had valuable life experience that could be "an asset" to professors and other students. Diane, like her descriptions of Margaret Stone, portrayed herself as wanting to learn for the joy of learning: "I've just always loved the academic setting and I love to learn." While many formerly incarcerated women may feel intimidated by the thought of attending college because they may be older than traditional students and perhaps they may begin college somewhat unfocused in their field of study, Diane had a model of a college student who was particularly admirable because of her age and her love of learning.

Diane was able to see herself as a college student because of her earlier experiences and her ongoing narrative that despite her crime and incarceration, she did in fact identify as a learner. When asked to describe what helped her envision herself as a college student, Diane reached back into a childhood memory of learning with her grandfather:

> My very first influence learning-wise was my grandfather, my Grandpa. When I was little, little, little, I learned to count matchsticks, playing cards, and I'd read the dictionary. He gave me a set of encyclopedias when I was five and just really instilled a love of learning. My childhood was very chaotic, but I just liked—this is gonna sound terrible—I like being smart. I like knowing the answers. Just him and then gosh, I guess it's just in my blood.

This encouragement and support from her grandfather helped her identify as a learner, and in addition, she storied herself as "being smart," and "knowing the answers." From a young age she saw that she could find pride and success in learning and knowing. Even within and perhaps despite the chaos of her childhood, she was able to narrate her childhood as one where she was able to learn and teach herself, even when others were not supportive. While her grandfather was supportive to her learning, Diane shared the story that her mother often undercut or mocked this identity, "I just—I've just always, always been stuck in the library and my mom would [say], 'You'd read the back of the cereal box,' and I said, 'I have, repeatedly. If there was anything else to read, I would.' I can't think of anything any more specific than that. It's just always been a part of who I am." Learning was always "just a part of" Diane's narrative of who she was. It was a story that she carried with her through her childhood, and it followed her into her incarceration and then when she was released and attended college. While this narrative could have been contradicted, destroyed or interrupted while she was incarcerated, because of several programs and experiences in prison, Diane reinforced her narrative identity of student.

Diane depended upon her narrative to help her through her incarceration. For example, she relied often upon reading and writing to help her not only pass the time, but also make sense of her past, and more destructive narratives that surrounded her crimes and addiction.

I have always been a writer and a journaler. I suppose journaling probably saved my life when I was first incarcerated. When I went into county jail, things were crazy and I was addicted to meth and I'd lost my children and my home. I had a therapist that—in this little, tiny, teeny, tiny town out there in the middle of nowhere, I had this woman that was just amazing. She encouraged me to write and I started writing on a yellow legal tablet and I just wrote, wrote, wrote, wrote. . . . It was the most amazing, cathartic experience I'd ever had and I kept writing.

While incarcerated there were a number of educational programs that Diane took advantage of. These reinforced her narrative of being a learner. We know that educational programs within prisons lower recidivism rates because they provide training for later employment and allow formerly incarcerated women to see themselves as productive during their time behind bars. At the same time, these programs give incarcerated people the identity of a learner, something that complicates and combats the negative social narratives connected to being an inmate. Diane took advantage of many of the education programs at the prison, explaining, "I had done a bunch of certifications. Some of them were fairly difficult. I knew that I could do the work there and hold my own with professional people in a bunch of different fields. That gave me confidence knowing that I could study again . . . and be able to take a test and to do well and to get these various certifications, I think really went a long way in giving me some confidence." Because of so many prison education programs, Diane was able to not only continue, but also build upon the narrative that began when she was young, that she "liked being smart" and "liked knowing the answers" as she did when she was a little girl learning with her grandfather, matchsticks, and encyclopedias. Even when the certifications were difficult, she was able to "hold her own." In other words, she wasn't only an inmate when she participated in the programs. She said that the certifications gave her confidence, but it is likely that the narrative she already held of herself as a learner gave her the confidence to begin these programs, and her success reinforced this confidence.

During her interviews, Diane took pride in describing the variety and number of programs in which she participated. It was clear that the narratives of her learning while incarcerated not only gave her confidence but also helped her survive and counter the opposing and destructive narratives that said she was merely a criminal, victim, addict, inmate.

I am a nationally certified playground safety inspector. . . . Bizarre but true. *[Chuckles]* I'm certified on a bunch of different power equipment, from a big front-end loader. I used to load salt trucks for the city. I ran a great big loader out at the recycling—where you drop the yard waste materials, recycling thingy, whatever it's called. The tree dump is what I called it. Just power equipment, I'm certified to run a forklift and . . . I am a [state] certified arborist. I am certified in landscape design. I got that when I was in prison. Just stuff, a whole bunch of different things.

The "stuff" that Diane describes as her training and certifications have real physical and cultural consequences and provided opportunities that ensured financial stability when she was released. In addition to the very real cultural capital and access to financial stability, Diane's training allowed her to see herself as a learner, as a worker, and as competent in a variety of skills and jobs. From being able to run a forklift to being certified to inspect playgrounds, Diane collected skills while incarcerated that positioned her as holding expertise and authority in areas she had not held before. Here she also found an identity beyond criminal, addict, and other culturally normalized narratives of incarcerated people. She gained confidence and a positive identity as well as marketable skills, "Yeah, I loved it. . . . They had a horticulture program. They did all the landscaping around the facility. Then at that time, they had all kinds of outreach stuff that they did for the state. We planted or grew and planted probably a thousand mums a year for the state capital. I designed and installed an herb garden at the [governor's mansion]."

The excitement she showed as she discussed her prison training became even more buoyant when she described what it was like to learn in college classes. She described herself as someone who just wanted to learn, "I had a terrible habit of soaking—I would just research, and research, and research, and research until I had no time left to write and to put things together. I would have to stop myself and say, 'Look, you know enough. . . . You've gathered enough information just to start writing.'" She described herself as a sponge and would engage in research not just to satisfy an assignment, but to actually satisfy her curiosity. She described working in the university library for hours up until the deadline for an assignment: "paper due on Monday. I'd be in there Sunday evening [until I] just felt like I was full, and it needed to get out . . . having it so sharp in my mind, so when I got to the computer or to a piece of paper, I knew pretty much what I wanted to do." Diane described her process of writing as a sort of filling herself up until she had to release the information onto the page. The assignments that other students might describe as drudgery or even busywork became exercises of filling herself up with knowledge and then sharing it. This is the excitement of being a learner, not just learning a skill to get a job. Though employment is crucial for justice-involved people, the ability to identify as a learner goes beyond the experiences of many correctional education programs, and very few formerly incarcerated women have the support and privilege to experience what Diane was able to.

The cultural narratives that identify and limit who belongs and can be successful in college is contradictory to that of the confining narratives of inmate or former inmate. However, because of the ways Diane was able to narrate her past experiences in childhood, in community college, and while incarcerated, she was able to tell a story of how and why she could be successful in college. She had personal and financial support from her partner which was critical to her degree completion. This, coupled with the fact that she was able to visualize herself as a successful college student, provided Diane with confidence and a sense of belonging that other formerly incarcerated women may lack. Diane was able to understand her college experience as just one more chapter in her long narrative of successful learning. And she was able to counteract the narrative portraying her as an outsider by retelling herself the story of Margaret Stone, a college student she could emulate as she began to story herself as a college student and graduate.

In the end, Diane was able to succeed in college through very tangible financial means, but also through the cementing of her identity as a learner based in her memories of Margaret Stone and her experiences as a learner while in prison. Her narrative identity was supported by those around her, and she was able to jump into learning without feeling the stigma or fear that many nontraditional college students might encounter. Her story is one that is unique because of how easily she was able to access and benefit from a college education. As we consider her story it becomes even clearer the many supports and cultural changes that must be put in place to allow other justice-involved people the access she found.

Chapter Eight

From Finding an Academic Home to "Feeling Untethered"

Diane was fortunate to have an atypical support system including the financial means to be a full-time college student. Diane's identity was firmly rooted in narratives of herself as a learner and student, and she was white, which carried its own cultural privilege. These three realities: the support she had outside of school, her white learner-centered identity, and faculty support made Diane's experience exceptional, and set her up for success. Even so, Diane's narratives also portrayed challenges and destructive sponsorships to her literacy practices and degree completion. As discussed previously, Deborah Brandt (1998) identifies literacy sponsorship as distinctly political in nature, and she acknowledges that sponsors can allow or withhold access to particular literacy experiences through which an individual may gain cultural and educational capital. On college campuses, constructive sponsorship can be many things—the accessibility of student support services, advising, and faculty support. Constructive sponsorship may also come in the form of an inclusive learning environment, which allows a student the feeling of belonging and authority over one's own learning. Some may argue that higher education serves primarily as a gatekeeper and only constructively sponsors a certain type of student. This is changing, and more and more colleges and universities are defining themselves through the lenses of social justice and access.

In response to increasing diversity within higher education, there has been a new focus recently on many campuses to improve access, equity, and inclusion to a more diverse student body. As an increasingly diverse student body brings to higher education various backgrounds, linguistic variations, political and religious affiliations, and sexual orientations, colleges and universities have been prompted to select content, assessment measures, and instructional strategies that acknowledge students' backgrounds as assets in the classroom. While very few faculty development programs have identified justice-involved people as making up a particular background in need of special inclusive practices, the movement of inclusive classroom practices and pedagogy overall holds promise to affect formerly incarcerated people's success in college classrooms. Training and professional development in diversity and inclusion in higher education has been influenced by a variety of disciplinary understandings including Universal Design/UDL (Burgstahler and Cory 2010; Silver et al. 1998), psychology (Aronson et al. 2002; Sue et al. 2007) and critical theory (Freire 2000; hooks 2014), among others. These disciplinary understandings should be broadened to also include research in criminal justice and correctional education. With those fields informing our work, higher education could choose to participate in the creation of a prison to school pipeline (Custer 2016, Halkovic 2014; Halkovic and Greene 2015; McTier, Santa-Ramirez, and McGuire 2017) as part of a university's social justice mission and interest in the public good.

Creation of more inclusive classrooms and campuses is an important moral endeavor that will help not only justice-involved people, but also other marginalized students. There is a growing population of students attending colleges and universities who do not fit into the narrative of the traditional college student. These students should be seen as providing benefits to college classrooms through their insight and experience rather than seen as creating burdens on campuses. Truly, institutions of higher education should embrace this work of social justice and community support by fully positioning themselves within a restorative prison to college pipeline. By looking closely at narratives of formerly incarcerated college students like Diane, college and university personnel can better understand their places in this path of possibility.

WHEN IDENTITY CONFLICTS WITH ONE'S FIELD OF STUDY

Upon entering the university, Diane planned to become an addictions counselor, so she could use her experience to help others. Because of her own less than positive experiences, Diane thought she would be especially positioned for this profession, and she shared that she used to plan for this while still in prison:

> Gosh. I remember coming in knowing exactly what it was that I wanted to do. I'd lay there in my bunk and I dreamed about helping people. After I'd gotten sober and my mind straight, I thought, "This is terrific. If I can help people do this, then that's what I wanna do," because I knew sometimes that I'd had less than successful experiences with counselors and probation people and that kinda thing before, when I was just going into the system. I'd been on proba-

tion for a while and I would go see my probation officer with dope in my pocket.

After becoming sober, Diane envisioned a path of giving back to others who faced addiction. Many college students who are formerly incarcerated see it as their responsibility to give back to society, and many of them go into the human services field. Halkovic and Greene (2015) found in their research that these students' "academic aspirations are often grounded in years of lived experiences and introspection, which provides them with detailed understandings of their responsibility to themselves and others." As a result of problematic advising, Diane enrolled in upper division human services classes her freshman year at Eastwood University. One of her professors was the chair of the Human Services department, so they met to discuss the addictions counseling program. After one meeting, Diane began to rethink this major, because of the way the field defined addiction, addicts, and recovery. "After having the department chair as a professor, then meeting with her, I was really disillusioned with the rigidity of her belief system. Lots of projection, and behavior I knew to be harmful as a former addict. I was looking for community as well, a place I felt comfortable being me, and that was not it." Diane's conversations with the chair led her to believe that her own experience with addiction would not be something that would benefit her in this career as she had previously imagined. The chair told Diane that she would have to always refer to herself as an addict and in continual recovery. This was the way, according to the chair, that the field of addictions counseling viewed addiction. Diane responded strongly against this idea because it would force her to renarrate her experience and her identity as recovered and moving beyond her addiction. "This realization that the system is so entrenched in just ugliness and stereotypical ideas of what an addict is or what they can be really set me back. The woman that was the department head at the time made a comment to me that I would always have to refer to myself as an addict in long-term recovery." Not only did Diane feel the narrative of addict was something she had moved beyond, she felt the idea of having to reclaim this narrative was "ugliness and stereotypical."

Diane rejected the label of addict. She didn't want to identify herself in that way. In her narrative of a student and then as a future addictions counselor, the identity of addict was inconsistent with and actually in opposition to her current and future identities. She quickly saw that if she did not embrace the identity of addict, she wouldn't be able to fit into the academic program. Therefore, she could not complete a degree in a field that was at odds with her own identity of being fully recovered.

I think it's such an individual experience. There's a billion addicts in the world. There are a billion ways to get clean and stay clean, but the premise is all the same. For them to tell me that I had to shoehorn myself into a particular mindset, or a stereotype, or a label in order to function in this particular career field choice, no, I wasn't going to do that.

This inconsistency between the disciplinary narrative of addiction and Diane's narrative of herself caused her to finally and completely give up her dream of being an addictions counselor. She rejected being shoehorned "into a particular mindset, or a stereotype, or a label." She rejected the label of addict for herself, and she would rather give up her career goals than embrace a narrative that she believed she had surpassed. She saw this as a narrative others wanted to force upon her and she resisted it. This resistance, while resulting in changing majors, also likely reinforced her narrative of herself as a student and a learner who had authority over her own educational path. She eventually was successful in college because she embraced more positive narratives positioning herself as powerful and in control of her destiny.

The temporal aspects of her narrative are significant. She storied her past as having overcome addiction and surpassing the label of addict. This storied past simultaneously provided a confidence to enroll in college and destroyed her ability to feel welcome within a field of study she wanted to enter. Instead of changing her identity as fully recovered to enter the addictions counseling field, she kept her identity and found a field where she would be welcomed. The commitment to her narrative of being a recovered addict allowed her to simultaneously embrace a narrative of her future as student and graduate though she was forced to revise the narrative of her future career.

FINDING A PLACE IN THE WRITING PROGRAM

As it became clear to Diane that she would not be able to continue upon the path to addiction counseling, she found general education courses where she was embraced wholly. In her English classes, she seemed to connect with her professors and she was not asked to try to fit into an outside narrative of her past, present, or future.

> At the same time [that I was speaking with the chair of Human Services], I had [Professor Halsey] for freshman comp and we just had got to be really super close. We came from the same community and the same group of people out in [Diane's home state]. She read my stuff and just—and then [Professor Gonzalez] at the same time. I had her the next semester and I realized this is what I wanted to do . . . that I could change my mind and just that realization that . . . being in college, if you have the right mindset, is as much realizing what you don't wanna do as what you do wanna do.

In the English department, she found professors who not only allowed her to claim an identity that didn't include the label of addict, but also who shared some history and geographical identity. Professor Halsey "came from the same community" and was able to connect with Diane in a way that transcended dominant narratives of inmate or addict. Diane realized that two of her English professors, Professor Halsey and Professor Gonzalez, embraced her without any outside assumptions. Through her experiences in their classes, she found that she had the power to not only decide to embrace a new major, but also reject her past narrative of her future as an addictions counselor. "I wasn't willing to force myself to get that [human services] degree with people like her [the department chair] over—in authority over me. . . . It just felt really ugly and it wasn't something I wanted to be a part of. I was welcomed so warmly by the English department here that I—it just was an amazing experience for me." Throughout her interviews, Diane continued to contrast the professors of the two departments. Human services faculty made her feel "ugly" and forced "an authority" over her that she resisted. On the other hand, faculty in the English department were "welcoming" and "warm." As a formerly incarcerated woman making the transition from a prison culture that imposed authority at every turn, and identified her as either invisible or evil, the differences between the Human Services and English departments were profound for Diane. Her success in transitioning to college occurred in part because she was able to identify herself firmly as a student who surmounted her past addictions and crimes. Here she was presented with two departments, one of which imposed a past identity she rejected. The other connected and welcomed the identity she presented. Her choice was straightforward and clear, and the decision to make the change was based as much on the professors she interacted with as the disciplinary content she would learn.

NARRATIVE OF SUPPORTIVE AND INCLUSIVE LEARNING COMMUNITY

After declaring English as her major, Diane had experiences that continued to reinforce that she had made the correct decision to leave the Human Services department. She told stories of many English department faculty encouraging her, complimenting her on her work, and providing special opportunities for her. She also described the department as a whole as an inclusive space where she was welcomed and nurtured: "I think that's what kept me coming back, was just that feeling of family and support and encouragement. I didn't wanna let people down here as much as I didn't wanna let myself down." Diane felt a responsibility to her professors, and this likely affected her retention and finally her graduation. "Yeah. I think just the continual involvement of my professors here, their willingness to promote me as a student and a person, to nominate me for things." Seeing her professors not only supported her, but "promoted" her, she told one story about a time when a well-known literature scholar and translator came to campus for a lecture. One of the English professors that was instrumental in bringing the scholar to campus invited Diane to join them for coffee following one of the lectures. She was also asked to escort the scholar across campus from one event to another. She said that this made her feel so fortunate and special as if she was welcomed into an inner circle. She continues to have a connection with the scholar on social media, and her professors have encouraged her to develop other similar connections outside of the department and campus.

Diane was singled out by her professors for many opportunities. She was nominated by a faculty member to attend a small group discussion at Eastwood University's president's home regarding how the institution could better serve nontraditional students. Diane narrated many of these connections as making a significant difference in the way she saw herself and the value others saw in her opinions. "Just to feel connected to people like that is so special. . . . If you do have to start over again, that's really good. It's cool. It's a new beginning. That's where miracles happen." Looking at Diane's story, it can seem that the attention of her professors, along with the inclusive nature of the English department did provide the context for certain miracles. However, Diane described other areas of exceptional support within Eastwood University.

SUPPORT IN GENERAL EDUCATION

The English department was not the only place where Diane felt she was supported. She identified two areas where she struggled in general education courses and provided stories of professors who went out of their way to help her find success. This is important to acknowledge that as a student she found connection and reinforcement in fields where she was not a major. For example, Diane described in detail her difficulties in math: "I struggled with math. . . . I fought it really, really, really hard 'cause I can do complex problems in my mind and add vast columns of numbers in my head. I couldn't sit there and do the work. Then when it got—came time for tests, I just—I couldn't do it. I had the most amazing math professor." Diane tested into a remedial math class; therefore, she was required to take additional math classes in order to satisfy graduation requirements. She described a great deal of frustration with math, and even said that she discussed her math classes with her therapist. She was not frustrated to the point of quitting, however, because of her math professor, Dr. Tyno, who spent time outside of class tutoring her until she found success. "He took time. He knew. . . he knew I wasn't stupid. He knew I wasn't dumb. He knew I was trying. He would tackle things from fourteen different directions. 'If you can't, okay, then let's try this. Let's try this.' I'd get it. . . I've never seen it before. Yeah. He really tried, and which I thought was amazing. I mean, and he did that with everybody."

Her math professor was not willing to give up on her and showed this by approaching her tutoring sessions "from fourteen different directions." He showed her that he believed she could learn, and that she "wasn't stupid." Dr. Tyno, by taking time with Diane, showed her she could succeed at even her most challenging courses, and he "did that for everybody." Though Diane didn't share whether or not her math professor was aware of her history as formerly incarcerated, it was clear that he provided an inclusive and supportive, student-centered teaching philosophy, and this played out in helping Diane, and likely many other students, succeed.

Diane noticed that she was helped in a way she didn't expect, and her narrative included that she was identified as special and was singled out because of her desire to learn. "I think I was given—I don't want to say a pass or a—I was given a boost. People, really, recognized that in me and gave me encouragement and maybe gave me opportunities that they wouldn't have given somebody else that wasn't as focused as what I was. [The faculty] embraced me in a way. I just sunk myself into the classes because I wanted to learn everything." She not only felt singled out, but also felt embraced by the faculty at Eastwood University. Faculty saw that she was focused and that she wanted to learn, so they provided extra help and extended opportunities to her. This in turn allowed Diane to further plunge into her studies and extend her learning beyond the campus.

CHALLENGES AND CONFLICTS IN HER COLLEGE CAREER

One setback that Diane had early in her college experience was when she worked with a general education advisor at Eastwood University. Like many universities, Eastwood provided general education advisors for students when they entered the institution, and then assigned them a faculty member in their field of study when they had declared their major. Effective advising is essential for all students, but it is especially critical for those who are already lacking financial and emotional support. For these students, poor advising becomes not merely an unfortunate irritation, but a substantial detriment to their college completion. Advising must go beyond course selection and include support as students negotiate the labyrinthine bureaucracies of academia. Many campuses are creating support programs for first generation college students or bridge programs to help underserved high school students transition successfully to a university context (Bir and Myrick 2015; Cabrera et al. 2013). Justice-involved people do not fit well within these programs as they are not coming from a high school, and while many may be first generation college students, their experiences are further complicated because of their myriad responsibilities that most college students do not yet carry.

GRADUATION: FROM "AN INCUBATOR OF GOOD THINGS" TO "FEELING UNTETHERED"

Diane's narratives of her college education included identification and descriptions of specific sponsorships: what allowed her to remain enrolled and complete her degree. Diane's narrative of transitioning from university student to graduate was in many ways much more complex and emotionally fraught than her transition from incarcerated person to student. Diane strongly identified as a student, and this identity was reinforced by her professors in the English department. She also had an unusually strong support system and financial support, allowing her to be a full-time student without holding a job to support herself. Throughout her college studies, she participated in volunteer opportunities that helped others who experienced addiction, abuse, or incarceration. For example, she regularly volunteered at a local prison, and served on several boards or committees focused upon correctional programs. It was through this work that Diane met Shanelle, who was the administrator of a domestic violence shelter called Beacon House in a nearby city. After a while, Shanelle offered Diane a job to work at the Beacon House.

> Monday evenings, I would go out to the prison and volunteer. We were at the meeting one cold winter evening and there was this beautiful silver-haired, immaculately dressed woman sitting there. I thought, "Oh, heavens. She's out of place." She was a new volunteer that was going in with the same group. We got to be really, really, really good friends. She's like my mom. . . . She was the administrator of the [Beacon House]. We got to know each other really well. She knew my story, and she wanted me to work for her. As my time was wrapping up [at school], she gave me a full-time position there but allowed me the time to do school, if that makes any sense. She wanted to help me be able to finish my last semester and work.

Since Diane was entering her last semester of coursework, she saw the job offer as a well-timed opportunity. It also offered her work for which she had a passion, and it would allow her to transition easily after graduation with a salary and benefits. Of course she jumped at the chance.

Unfortunately, this job turned out to be something that was the first piece in a perfect storm of events that created chaos in Diane's last semester. The job pulled Diane away from campus in unexpected ways and also turned out to be a toxic environment within which to work. Because of her work responsibilities, Diane elected to take mainly online courses to complete the credits she needed for her degree. It soon became clear to Diane that online coursework was nothing like her experience of learning in a face-to-face classroom setting. She described her coursework as "horrible," and said it was her "worst semester." She said when she thought about her last semester, the memory of it just "made her sad." Diane's narrative of this worst semester included not only her new job and the stress of working with domestic violence survivors and their children, but also her inability to come to classes on campus. "I just failed to make those connections that I like to make. I was just too busy, and I hated it. Then going to work there triggered every bad thing."

Adding to the perfect storm of this final semester, Diane was assaulted while engaged in her regular volunteer work at the prison. Suddenly, Diane was dealing with trauma from the assault, she was regularly triggered by the work she was doing at the domestic violence center, and her connection and community at the university was distressingly absent. "I would pull up to [Beacon House] and I would sit out there and I would have panic attacks in the parking lot." She described this semester as a great disappointment. While she was happy she was able to finish, she didn't have a feeling of accomplishment or satisfaction she had hoped to experience. Instead, she finished weakly, dragging herself across the finish line.

Diane was not about to let circumstances derail her although she readily admitted that she was not able to study or otherwise actively engage in her classes to the extent that she had in earlier semesters. Here, where Diane had earlier described the university as "an incubator" that helped her to grow and birth new ideas and insights, she had lost her connection with that feeling of sustenance.

Within Diane's narrative of her last semester, other identities crowded out her student-identity. Because of her assault, she once again was pulled into the identity of a victim/survivor; this was an identity that she had worked hard to overcome. The work at the domestic abuse center not only triggered past traumas, she was once again in a position in which the person in authority over her created an unhealthy work environment through problematic management practices. Diane was suddenly in a position where she lacked control of her own work and it paralleled what she experienced in prison.

Other students go through traumatic events and feelings of disconnection and doubt without the knowledge of their professors, and the ways they story this experience and integrate it into their identities can either interfere with or strengthen their resolve to complete their degrees. Many students, like Diane, also have jobs off campus that they have to balance with their studies. Online coursework is often a solution for students who have complicated schedules and responsibilities, or who are geographically unable to attend on-campus coursework. While online coursework can provide access to students who would otherwise be unable to enroll in college classes, it should be noted that these students do not have access to the same experiences of connection, mentoring, and support that on-campus students experience. Here is the one point in her college career when Diane's experience might be closer to other formerly incarcerated women who have to work and who are still negotiating their student identities and dealing with current and past traumas.

While any college student has mixed feelings during their last semester before graduation, Diane found that her college experience ended in disconnection and trauma. Diane described so much of her early experience as a college student as full of possibility and growth, and she narrated her own identity solidly as a college student. The ending of her college career greatly contrasted with her earlier narratives and coincided with other endings and this forced her to doubt her idea of who she was and her place in the world. When Diane described how she felt following her graduation, instead of this time being one of pride in her success and looking forward to an exciting and promising future, it was a time of disconnection and uncertainty:

> Yeah. Just feeling really untethered and unfulfilled. It sounds weird. . . . Gosh, I just loved it [at the university]. Gosh. Just that last semester of school here was just such a storm of so many different things. In a way, I was glad to be done, because I knew that it was getting to the point where I really needed to focus on myself. I really started having a mental health crisis. . . . It was a tough time, but it really—there were so many outside circumstances. . . . Life had just become a lot at that time . . . my daughter left, and the assault, and my work with the domestic violence center was too much. I was trying to figure out who I was and what I was gonna do with my life.
>
> A lot of things came to an end at this particular—right there at that time. I really didn't know who I was or what I was supposed to be doing. It was this and all my volunteer work and my work in the world and my idea of motherhood and being older, and I was going through menopause. I'll never be a mom again.
>
> I'll never again—just watching these parts of myself die away and not knowing what there was underneath has taken me—well, four years, five years, six years to figure it out. I'll always be figuring it out. I think I'm really learning to love myself. That was something that I didn't do through all that process. I wasn't kind and I wasn't gentle with myself. I wish I would've been *[chuckles]*.

Diane's identity as a student was so strong and her connections to those at the university were so substantial and so informing of her view on the world, that graduation, in addition to other events of the time, introduced a series of doubts. Diane described watching parts of herself "die away," and certainly one of those parts was her identity as a student.

Most formerly incarcerated women will need to work and have other responsibilities with children and other family members. They will have financial challenges both to support themselves and their children. As they juggle these obligations, they must also develop strong student identities and connections to the campus in order to succeed. Many may try to take classes online or otherwise attend classes without constructively connecting to the university community. Despite all her challenges during her last semester, Diane was able to finish because she felt she was supported and didn't want to let anyone down. Few formerly incarcerated women have this sort of sponsorship. It is important to recognize that success in reentry and a successful transition from prison to college doesn't always depend upon skill level. It is about so many other issues such as financial support, parenting responsibilities, work schedule, stigma, and self-identity. Success also has much to do with the sponsors who will meet justice-involved people at the university gates and whether they will be constructive guides or destructive gatekeepers.

Diane's selection of an English major was not in her original plans, but because she was able to find a community in the English department, she was able to learn and integrate many important lessons, including how to better connect with others and being able to ask and answer her own questions. She described what she learned from her college experience: "Yeah, in that way of making connections, building relationships. In a tangible way, my writing has been hugely helpful. Having the ability to know—be able to feel what people need to hear and respond in that way, in an authentic way, I think to be able to think analytically, to question things, to question everything. I knew that before, but that really reinforced it here and being able to do different types of research." Diane also described learning about using technology in an effective way as part of her English degree:

> When I left college in 1986, we still used an IBM Selectric typewriter *[chuckles]*. I did research literally from books in the library and a card catalogue. Then I get back here, and obviously thirty—literally thirty years later, everything had changed, technology-wise and information. I mean, it was just incredible the difference. How lucky kids are today, people are today, to be in school compared to the way it was in 1986. You have everything at your fingertips—literally, everything, if you just know how to use it and to use it well. . . I think, "Okay, gosh. That's it." Now in running my business, I have a better knowledge of how to find information and what to do with that information, how to organize my writing, how to communicate with clients and banks and the government. Just being confident in your ability to communicate, I think is—in my ability to communicate—I can't necessarily get the right words all the time. I guess that's why I write *[chuckles]* and hard edit. Yeah.

After graduation, Diane did not go on to support herself as a writer. She continued to volunteer and worked with her husband to build their tree trimming business. However, the lessons learned in her college education went beyond the skill sets that one might believe would come with a degree in

English. Her education was not merely preparation for a very particular career. Instead she learned skills of effective communication and methods of critical and creative thinking. She also learned about herself and grew in confidence as she put more years and experiences between her present and her past incarceration. Diane explained that though she is not supporting herself as a writer, she is constantly using her degree:

> Oh, golly. [I use my degree] in every way *[chuckles]*. It's weird. I have my college degree. Well, it's informed everything, how I see the world, just the people that I've met. Probably that more than anything, the people that I continue to be friends with that have influenced my life and the way I see things . . . and just people having the bravery to embrace themselves fully and authentically. . . . Some of the students that I went to school with, seeing what they're doing in the world, that we're fortunate and we have a responsibility to do things to make the world a better place. [The university] is a huge springboard. I mean, like an incubator for good things for me.

Diane also described how she continues to write for herself, and currently is involved in a writers group that meets regularly to critique each other's work. When describing the writing she does today, she replied,

> Gosh. I love to write just about everything. Poetry, structured and otherwise, lots of memoir, short stories, book reviews and literary comparison. I am starting a cookbook for my daughters and grands, full of pictures and stories. I am going to write about my women, grandmothers, and aunts and cousins who live before me (sic). I also see documenting my recovery and process some day. I have written to save myself, quite literally. I write to make sense of the past, or try to. I write to transmute pain and trauma, and always have, long before knowing what I was doing. I write for fun and enjoyment too.

Though Diane isn't using her writing degree to support herself financially, it is clear she is using it to support herself emotionally and mentally. Her education and her writing helped her to "save" herself and "make sense of the past." The literacy sponsorship of her professors not only helped Diane obtain a college degree, but it also provided her with skills, knowledge, and confidence to use what she has learned to cement her identity and overcome stigma. Here we see one perfect example of how literacy sponsorship provides social capital for formerly incarcerated women. Diane has changed the experience of her former incarceration into something that empowered and connected her rather than something that stigmatized and separated her.

Chapter Nine

Opening the Gates

Narratives from Diane's Professors

Diane's success at Eastwood University had much to do with her own circumstances, with luck that she was in a financial and personal position to be supported as she studied. Besides luck though, Diane was also successful because she narrated an identity in which she was a learner and a student. While her identity included her past incarceration, she narrated this experience in ways that portrayed it as advantageous to her college goals. She wasn't worn down by the stigma that many justice-involved women carry, at least while she was in the classroom. Diane was fortunate to have a number of professors in the English department at Eastwood University who served as constructive literacy sponsors. These professors narrated Diane as a student they admired and enjoyed teaching. Their narratives often aligned with those Diane told of herself, so they not only supported her in the classroom as faculty traditionally do, but they also reinforced the narrative that Diane's past was advantageous to her studies as an English major. As literacy sponsors, the faculty members, Justine, Max, and Kevin, also provided support and expertise to help Diane access academic literacies, and the complex discourse situation of higher education.

Academic literacies are inherently exclusionary, but with the sponsorship of astute and accommodating faculty, students can be provided access to these multiple academic literacies and admitted into the discourse community that previously seemed inaccessible. The New London Group published a paper in 1996 identifying "multiliteracies" as a new way for classroom teachers to approach literacy instruction. Instead of focusing upon "literacy" as a single pinnacle that one must reach in order to communicate through reading and writing within society, the New London Group saw literacy in the plural, and as socially constructed. Therefore, multiple social groups demand multiple summits one might reach and interact within, and each of these summits are regulated, accessed, and interact with each other through varied levels of power and control over their speakers and readers and among those who are fluent in other literacies. Some literacies are clearly dominant in a culture, and some are closed but to a very small group. Access to and fluency within multiple literacies provide individuals with flexibility to communicate across groups and provide them with access and power from which they may otherwise be prohibited. The New London Group (1996) identified the difference between literacy and multiliteracies as this:

> What we might term "mere literacy" remains centered on language only, and usually on a singular national form of language at that, which is conceived as a stable system based on rules such as mastering sound-letter correspondence. This is based upon the assumption that we can discern and describe correct usage. Such a view of language will characteristically translate into a more or less authoritarian kind of pedagogy. A pedagogy of multiliteracies, by contrast, focuses on modes of representation much broader than language alone. These differ according to culture and context, and have specific cognitive, cultural, and social effects. . . . Multiliteracies also create a different kind of pedagogy, one in which language and other modes of meaning are dynamic representational resources, constantly being remade by their users as they work to achieve their various cultural purposes. (64)

This identification of multiple literacies that one can move in and out of and negotiate and combine has great implications not only in teaching, but also in how we see language and communication as tied up with politics, oppression, access, and all other areas where people can be welcomed into or excluded from a group or experience. It has implications regarding how we use language to separate, control, isolate, or punish individuals whose literacies do not match those in power.

The literacy expectations of higher education are especially fraught with power dynamics, requiring students to become quickly knowledgeable about how to read and write within academia. While it has been shown that more affluent high schools better prepare students to read and write within academic discourses, many students who come to our college classrooms find the ways we write and the texts we read as foreign and confusing, and faculty when faced with these students are at best often confounded by how to help these students become fluent in academic discourse. At worst, faculty write off students as lacking intelligence or being lazy rather than considering they have never been introduced to the literacy in which they are now expected to show fluency. To make this process even more confounding for students, they are expected to also learn the subtleties of different and more specialized literacies of the different disciplines in which they engage. A student within one semester may possibly learn to communicate as a poet, a scientist, and a historian, a process which often leaves students to see themselves as "strangers in a strange land" (McCarthy 1987), continually confounded by the changing rules which seem to be based on the whim of each particular professor. David Bartholomae (1986) described this process of students learning to write in college as "inventing the university" within their minds. As students work to learn the disciplinary content, they must also imagine themselves as a part of the discourse community that communicates the content through very specific and value-laden ways,

> The students have to appropriate (or be appropriated by) a specialized discourse, and they have to do this as though they were easily and comfortably one with their audience, as though they were members of the academy, or historians or anthropologists or economists; they have to invent the university by assembling and mimicking its language, finding some compromise between idiosyncrasy, a personal history, and the requirements of convention, the history of a discipline. They must learn to speak our language. Or they must dare to speak it, or to carry off the bluff, since speaking and writing will most certainly be required long before the skill is "learned." (4–5)

> The writer must get inside of a discourse he can only partially imagine. The act of constructing a sentence, then, becomes something like an act of transcription, where the voice on the tape unexpectedly fades away and becomes inaudible. (19)

This can be a daunting task for any student, but those who are already marginalized, and whose home literacies are already devalued within societal norms often find themselves even further alienated and stigmatized as their classroom communication missteps become conflated as portraying a lack of intelligence, care, or work ethic. Students come to believe that they just aren't cut out for college, or they carry a deficit that cannot be overcome. It is up to faculty across disciplines in higher education to help these students in particular unlock and lay visible the subtleties of academic discourse. This is a pedagogical act and also a political act of providing access to groups who have been marginalized and historically excluded from higher education.

Thankfully, over the last two decades, higher education has become more focused upon student-centered pedagogies as more diverse students have enrolled in colleges and universities. This new focus also comes alongside a body of research that shows how the best college professors provide individualized attention for students. Whereas a professor's role in the past was a disconnected lecturer or a "sage on the stage" who deposited information into what was assumed to be the empty heads of students (Freire 2000), it is clear now that students are more engaged in their learning when faculty provide learning activities that are connected to the individual learners in each particular classroom, their rates of learning, and their particular needs. Rather than seeing students as merely members of a homogenous group, student-centered learning strategies are those that engage students in the learning process by providing meaningful activities that require students to reflect on their learning. Substantial research, including work by Maryellen Weimer on *Learner-Centered Teaching* (2002) and Ken Bain's study, *What the Best College Teachers Do* (2004), demonstrate that various forms of student-centered learning contribute to positive student outcomes. These outcomes include the following: deep, conceptual learning; active construction of knowledge; development of personal ownership of learning; and improved student attitudes and opinions about their learning. In this way, professors could also more easily step into the role of constructive sponsor (Brandt 1998) who might provide access to the unique literacy constructs and expectations of higher education.

Sponsorship between a professor and student in higher education can take place through four different interconnected roles. First, as already mentioned, a professor can sponsor a student through classroom instruction, providing an inclusive learning environment where the student is engaged. Second, sponsorship can occur through academic advising. Especially for first generation students, it can be extremely disorienting to face the myriad bureaucracies of the university. Research has shown that the quality of advising a first generation college student received was directly related to whether or not they persisted (Swecker, Fifolt, and Searby 2013). Third, sponsorship occurs through the teaching that takes place outside the classroom. When a professor meets one on one to tutor or conference with a student, it can provide special connection to the institution and clarification of the course content that may not happen during a regular class period. Finally, a professor can mentor a student by sharing particular opportunities, events, or materials to which the student would not regularly have access. The professors in this study identified themselves in these roles of constructive sponsorship for Diane. Every professor did not inhabit all the roles, but Diane was sponsored by these faculty through the four roles amongst the various relationships she had while a student.

DIANE'S FACULTY SPONSORSHIPS

During the interviews with three of Diane's English professors, it was clear that the three professors had varied levels of clarity regarding their memories of Diane. Justine, a literature professor and Diane's academic advisor, in preparation for the interview, reviewed her past calendars and identified how many times and on what dates they had met for advising sessions. She also looked up the class she taught in which Diane was a student. She brought this information with her to the interview. Kevin also looked up past documentation of his work with Diane. He had retained electronic copies of her work as well as his responses to drafts of her writing, so he reviewed these artifacts before the interview and following the interview shared his written responses to be used as artifacts for data analysis. Max did not prepare in the same ways that Justine and Kevin did, so his interview originated from his memories alone. When asked to participate in the interviews, these three participants were not directed in any way to review past documents, calendars, or the like. Justine and Kevin elected to do this on their own to help jog their memories of interactions with Diane.

Both Justine and Kevin also mentioned that they continued to be in touch with Diane after her graduation. Justine, for example, said she made an effort to support past students especially if they were involved in local businesses, so since her graduation, Justine had hired Diane and her husband to do some tree trimming work on her property. Kevin also mentioned that he was in touch sporadically with Diane because she regularly worked with his father. In these ways, Justine and Kevin's more recent interactions with Diane may also have colored their views of her and may affect their narratives of Diane and her success.

Each of the professors provided narratives of the way they saw Diane as a student and in Justine's case, also as an advisee. Each narrative shared below is constructed to clearly portray Justine's, Max's, and Kevin's individual storied perceptions of Diane.

Justine, Narratives from Her Relationship as Advisor and Professor

Justine was assigned to be Diane's academic adviser when she declared English as a major. Even though Diane had taken classes in human services as she worked toward that degree, Justine said she was never formally made aware that Diane had changed majors or that she had originally planned to study something other than creative writing. Justine met with Diane each semester for six semesters and was also Diane's professor in a literature survey class. Justine described Diane as an enjoyable and responsible advisee. She also described her as a strong student with original ideas.

As her advisor, Justine saw Diane as a student who was professional and affable. Justine said that she recalled enjoying their advising meetings and the interaction she had with Diane:

> What I really liked with advising meetings is when the student asks a lot of questions, and it's clear that they want to show you what they're interested in, and then you help them find classes that are relevant to their interests, rather than just a five minute, "Here's my required classes," or something; she was, definitely, one of [the students who showed an interest]. I got a good sense of

her academic interests, I should say, from those meetings. She was always on
time; I remember that, and very polite, but also very warm and friendly.

Diane was engaged and interested in discussing the possibilities for her
course schedules. At the same time, Justine sensed that Diane had struggled
in the past and that may have been what was driving her to be so organized
and focused in their advising sessions. "She was very much on track, keeping
track of all the classes she still needed; she wanted to get done quickly, but
she was very responsible about planning all of this. . . . I always had the sense
that, maybe in the past, there had been a challenge, but that now she was
really focused on getting done. . . . I actually admire her even more for
coming back from what I already knew was a very difficult place." Even
though Justine sensed that Diane had worked through past challenges, it was
not something that she described as a detriment. Rather, past challenges were
discussed as possibly a reason that Diane was now such a driven and responsible student. Diane wanted to complete her degree quickly and efficiently,
and as her advisor, Justine appreciated this effort and impulse to do so.

As her instructor, Justine also simultaneously appreciated Diane and wondered about her personal life or past. Justine described Diane's work as solid
and imaginative, yet she also recalled that there were a number of times when
Diane missed class or was late in turning in her work. Justine sensed this was
due to other responsibilities outside of school, and remembered Diane explaining some absences were because of volunteer work:

> I do remember that she was very good about checking in with me. From her
> emails, it sounded like she felt guilty when she couldn't submit something on
> time. Yeah, very much so. I also have to say, with some students, I'm some-
> times worried that they may never turn something in, but I never worried about
> Diane.
>   I did want to mention . . . I told you she would email me about her
> upcoming absences. She always explained what it was about. I went back,
> because I wanted to remember what some of the things were in my emails, and
> one was about a court hearing to advocate for two ladies from a shelter. One
> was a presentation at [unintelligible] with her Criminal Justice class. One was
> another one about helping at the shelter. . . . I was very much aware, both as
> her advisor, and her instructor, that she was very active in helping women that
> she identified with, based on what she told me, that had very similar struggles.

The information that Diane shared about her personal life seemed to make
sense in the context of her academic interests as well. Justine recalled that
Diane was interested in taking courses or writing papers that dealt with issues
of gender and class.

> At that time, at least, she seemed very interested—even in our class discus-
> sions, she was very interested in Women's Studies, and in literature by and

about women's experiences. I did get a sense of that. Beyond that, I think she was quite interested, in terms of time periods, especially in Modernism; I think she was interested in that. I think that, in terms of her general education classes, I think she often was interested in gender, and societal issues, like social class, gender, race. I did get that impression.

Justine was the only one of the three professors interviewed who said she had not been aware of Diane's incarceration. When this was discussed in the interview, Justine said that it made sense based on what she knew of Diane and what Diane had shared about her past. Justine was not surprised by this information.

> In preparation for the interview, I was trying to think back, and if she ever did [tell me about her incarceration], I just never consciously knew it. What she did share with me—I do remember that early on in our advising meetings, not in class—she did share with me that she had a hard past, that she struggled. I think she said she was, at one point, without a place of residence, and maybe even lived at a shelter. She did tell me that she struggled with addiction, with, specifically, drug addiction, in the past. By the time she became my advisee, she even talked to me about—maybe it came up in talking about some of the course content in our advising meeting, or something. She said that she's in a wonderful relationship with her now-spouse. Actually, I do not remember that she told me she was incarcerated.

Justine described her knowledge of Diane's past struggles, her homelessness, and her addiction in a fairly nonchalant way. It was a piece of Diane's past, but it wasn't necessarily something that Justine saw as Diane's main identity or something that would complicate her studies. Rather, these details were only shared when Justine was prompted in the interview to explain what she knew of Diane's incarceration. These details were not the first nor were they the most prominent in Justine's memories of Diane as a student and advisee. With more prompting, Justine explained that she did not consciously think about how Diane's past might affect her studies:

> Everything else that she related—one could make an assumption [that she'd been incarcerated]—but I never consciously did, just that there was a time when she had really bad relationships with her family, and so on, and struggled with drug addiction, and then she was at a shelter. I believe there was some fear of domestic violence, and so on. . . . No, it actually doesn't surprise me at all. I do remember when she first told me about some of the drug addiction, and some of the really bad things, that she was homeless . . . I think, at that point, I remember being somewhat surprised, not negatively, just surprised, because the person in front of me, that I had developed an advising relationship with, was so professional. It seemed so distant. I think if there was any surprise, it was maybe then, but now I'm not. It doesn't change at all, how I see her.

As both her professor and her advisor, Justine narrated Diane in supportive ways, and also provided narratives that pushed against the traditional narratives of the "successful college student." Justine did not see Diane in a negative light, even when she brought up some negative events in her past. Justine still considered Diane to be professional, and since they had established a positive working relationship, any stigma that may have followed Diane was nonexistent in Justine's mind. Justine saw "the person in front of [her]" and the past, though surprising, didn't change the narrative she'd crafted to identify who Diane was and the type of student she could become.

Max: Connecting Theory to Diane's Past

Max met Diane when she was in his literary criticism class about midway through her studies. His sponsorship of Diane was mainly as her professor and also through conferences and conversations after class. Max recalled that when Diane was enrolled in his class he did not have any other classes following, so it was often convenient to talk after class, either in the hall or his office. The class read and discussed literary theory, and Max saw Diane at first as a student who would sit back and judge the classroom situation before jumping in. He said that he really didn't get to know her well until some time had passed in the semester: "It seems to me that she was pretty quiet at first. . . . She was a little bit careful [laughter] so she didn't particularly stand out at first. As the semester went on and she built up more trust, then she felt more comfortable talking in class. I think it also helped that the class was good, so she felt more comfortable that way too." Her work as a student was of a high quality, but it was clear to Max that Diane wasn't there to just make the grades, but rather to learn. She was intrinsically motivated, and sometimes that meant that she didn't fulfill assignments. "The work that she did was good, but she didn't do all of it. I remember knowing that at the time. . . . I remember thinking that she really wasn't there. It wasn't about the grades. It wasn't about [laughter] performing. It was about actually learning something, which I could go with that." Max's description complements Justine's views that Diane was present and wanted to learn, but wasn't in class to perform in the ways that many students do. She would turn in quite a bit of late work for Justine, and she would turn in incomplete work for Max. Even so, these professors weren't put off by what some might describe as a less than stellar academic performance. They enjoyed working with her and saw that she cared about learning. Max described her in this way:

> I would probably—in a scientific way I'd have to describe her as mediocre as a student, but mediocre in terms of grades. I don't want to say mediocre as a student. Mediocre in terms of grades, but certainly engaged and interested, and all those things that are really important she was very good at. . . . Yeah. I think it's part of her being a non-traditional student. I don't just think that it's just

the incarceration. I think that she knew what she wanted out of her schooling, and it wasn't necessarily the grades.

In his narratives of Diane, Max differentiated between a good student "in terms of grades" and in terms of "all those things that are really important." This attitude created a positive relationship between Max and Diane. Max identified and respected Diane's abilities even though she didn't always make the grade. He provided support and sponsorship for Diane to continue to participate and learn even though she didn't necessarily fit into the traditional narrative of how a "good student" performs.

The narrative of Diane's advantages as a nontraditional student also appears throughout Max's discussion. His narrative both complements and counters Diane's own personal narrative of seeing herself as different from the students around her primarily because she was older and had different experiences. The narrative of the nontraditional student includes the fact that Diane was intrinsically motivated. She did care about learning, but she did not necessarily care about performing, or as Max stated several times in his interview, she didn't care about grades and "she knew what she wanted." In many ways, Diane was nontraditional not only in age but also in the ways she approached learning. She took control of her learning, and instead of feeling threatened or uncomfortable with this, Max said that he "appreciated" that she did this:

> Also, the non-traditional student thing, where she was willing to be—what do I want to say? She was willing to get what she wanted out of the class, whether or not that aligned with what the class [laughs] was about. I think that's clear. . . . I appreciated that. I think that's a good thing. . . . You get people who've been through various life issues, including incarceration. She's not the only student. I hadn't really processed that before. . . .Well, I think that most of the people we deal with are eighteen- and twenty-year-olds who almost all of them have not had many life experiences. For somebody to come in and—with all this baggage is a really—I think that's non-traditional students in general. They bring more life experiences to the classroom. I'm always interested in the way that people can bring their own experiences to the classroom. I don't want to say I thought that her incarceration *[laughs]* was a good thing. . . . Clearly not, but it gives her a perspective that I thought was interesting and neat. I knew that she could bring something to her own work because of it. Yeah. As I say, I don't want to make that sound like a good thing, but I think that you could get positive things from that.

Unlike her relationship with Justine, Diane discussed her incarceration regularly with Max. These conversations began a few weeks into the semester after reading Michel Foucault's *Discipline and Punish: The Birth of the Prison*. Max recalls that this reading especially provided much content for their conversations.

I don't know whether I knew about her incarceration before that. Certainly that book gave her plenty to talk about and plenty to think about. Then she could come to me and say, "Well, I know something about this because I've been there." I think during the discussion of Foucault . . . she was willing to talk about that, and to use some of those experiences to talk about Foucault in particular. . . . The incarceration clearly affected her a lot, and she was really clear about trying to recover from that.

Through their conversations, Diane was able to say, "I know something about this," and connect her own experiences to a challenging theoretical text. She was able to bring the gifts (Halkovic and Greene 2015) of her incarceration to a college classroom and provide context and practical lived observations to Foucault's theory. Max saw through her discussion of Foucault how the incarceration had affected her and how she was "trying to recover." Like Justine, he didn't see her past as a detriment, rather something that she was working through and that may affect her work as a student, but not necessarily in a negative way. And in the case of his literary criticism class and the study of Foucault, her incarceration provided a unique benefit of entering the text through firsthand experience. Later, as they talked more after class, Max described that Diane began to open up more and they had fairly regular conversations. He said those conversations "were mostly about the incarceration. Mostly about that. That became a touchstone for us."

These conversations also helped him see Diane in a different light and perhaps in a clearer light, but he stated that knowing she had been incarcerated didn't change the way he saw her or her work in his class. At the same time, he described that knowledge as becoming a "touchstone" that provided an entry point for other conversations.

I don't think that everybody in that situation would be forthcoming about it. It is nice to know information like that about students. I do [think it is good to know this about students]. Yeah. In classes of twenty, twenty-five students it's easy for people to become anonymous, and the fact that I remembered Diane and *[laughs]*. All this may have been a really tough experience, but it made her an interesting person.

He saw his knowledge of her background merely as something that "made her an interesting person" and it kept her from being "anonymous" in his class of twenty to twenty-five students. The experience did not cause him to see her as a problematic student, nor did the experience carry stigma. It was something out of the ordinary. Max also mentioned that it appeared that Diane was trying to process her past, and that she didn't try to hide it. Perhaps it was the course content that allowed her to take a more academic look at her past. Max described it in this way, "I think that's maybe one of the main things that I remember, is that she was clearly trying to process this whole experience and understand it and do something with it and move beyond it. Also not deny it and just act like it never happened." While Justine knew some about Diane's past, but not her incarceration, Max was quite aware of it and it became a part of their conversations connected to the class readings. Her incarceration became a beneficial extension to the materials he taught. The third professor, Kevin, had a slightly different take on her past and how he saw it connected to her coursework.

Kevin: Creativity, Imagination, and Gratitude

Kevin had Diane in two different creative writing classes, and he was the only one of Diane's writing professors who was interviewed. Since his classes were focused upon creative writing, the format required students to share their own writing with classmates. Within this structure, students and the professor get to know each other fairly well through the writing presented and critiqued. Besides the interview, Kevin also shared a number of his written commentaries on Diane's work, which he had typed and kept in digital files on his computer.

Like both Justine and Max, Kevin's narrative focused primarily upon Diane as a nontraditional student rather than her identify as a formerly incarcerated person:

> I think that she began to distinguish herself from the others. I don't mean that in a qualitative way, but just kind of in my mind, set herself apart by the quality of her insights and comments that she offered in class. I was aware that she was a nontraditional student older than most of her peers in the class, and that when you're first getting to know students, superficial things like that help you connect to memory who they are and things like that.

He also stated that seeing her as a nontraditional student was a first impression that helped him distinguish her from others in the class. However, her status as a nontraditional student was "superficial," so it was a way to begin to distinguish her from other students in the class, but eventually it became a less important part of who she was. Kevin's narrative portrayed Diane as a strong student who actively participated in class.

> I think from fairly early in the first semester I had an emerging strong, very positive impression of her. She seemed really always to be enjoying the class and be grateful to be there. She participated a lot, as I recall. Never in an intrusive way or in the way that makes it all about her. She just always had really good things to say, I think. Really insightful readings and the poems, really astute, genuinely helpful comments on her classmates' work. Yeah, she was just a model student in that respect. I keep coming back to these words of gratitude and enthusiasm.

Kevin's narrative not only portrayed Diane as a strong student, but as a "model student" which is slightly different from how Justine and Max described her. Throughout Kevin's narrative he describes Diane as feeling "gratitude" for being able to be in class, and he said that her successful performance in class originated from these feelings of gratitude. She was enthusiastic because she felt grateful to be there. She actively participated in class because she was grateful to be there.

> She seemed so grateful for the opportunity to be having these conversations and so enthusiastic about the subject and got along well with everybody. There didn't seem to be a noticeable—the age gap in between her and other students didn't create any kind of a barrier between them or anything like that. Not because she was trying to act younger. You know what I mean like that, but she just fit seamlessly into the conversations, and just sowed goodwill with everything that you said. . . . I think that she's up there with the best students that I've ever had, and by virtue of being older and more mature and more experienced than the typical student, I think that that benefited her too. She was just a dream student. The positive attitude contributed to that significantly. Just the sense that she was grateful to be in class every day.

In the above quotation, Kevin used the word grateful twice, and he repeated this throughout his interview. Her gratitude was a benefit to both her and the other students.

Kevin did identify Diane's past incarceration as part of her identity, but he also did not see it necessarily as a deficit. As we finished up our interview, Kevin asked to share one more story that he thought was important. He then renarrated a story that Diane had once told him. He was particularly touched by this story. It is poignant because his telling shows that he was trying to see Diane's past through her own eyes. A story she shared with him about her incarceration was one he chose to share, and in some ways, this story was more vivid in his mind than stories of her as a student in his classroom.

> There's one especially vivid story that she told me that I feel like, I don't know, it's a story that I think of when I think of her. She said that when she was incarcerated she was in a facility that was adjacent to a school that her daughter attended. She had a window where she could see her daughter out at recess. You can see why that stayed with me.

This story created a poignant picture of loss and of separation and of yearning. It is also the story of a parent. Kevin, who had his own children, could empathize with Diane watching her daughter but being unable to be with her or even communicate with her. Kevin described this story as one that touched him, but it also constructed his understanding of Diane as a mother and as someone who had suffered and was given another chance.

It's a really memorable story obviously and a heart-wrenching story, but also I think that story informs my understanding of her [in] the sense that if you've been there and have gotten beyond that to where she is now, then every day would seem like this incredible gift to not be squandered. Just the perspective you would have about your life and the opportunities that you've been given would be so much more sophisticated than the typical college student could possibly have or even the typical college professor could possibly have.

Kevin's narrative of Diane portrayed her as having a "sophisticated" view of the world that was beyond other college students. This set her apart from the other students with which he worked, and it also forced him to see Diane's perspective as one that was beyond his own and other "typical college professors." It was a perspective that he could ponder and learn from. When asked if his knowledge of her incarceration affected how he saw her as a student, he replied:

That's I think part of the reason that the word gratitude keeps coming back to me. The sense that there's been this moment of absolute rock bottom, but also, I mean that specific image of her being able to look out and see her daughter at recess and she's right there and yet unreachable. I'm literally seeing what I'm missing out on right now. . . . It must have [affected how I saw her as a student]. I don't know how it could not. I don't know that it changed the way that I worked with her necessarily. I think it just deepened my appreciation for her and informed my understanding of the—as a teacher that we get these periodic reminders of the incredible journey that some student has been on that has brought them into our classroom. It's always humbling. It's always like, oh, I had you in my mind as kind of two dimensional. I now realize, and you've just popped into three dimensions. . . . I don't know that I ever had a two dimensional view of Diane, but it certainly deepened and complicated my appreciation of her.

Like Max, Kevin expressed that knowing Diane's background allowed him to see her as different from his other students, but also as one who "popped into three dimensions" and who humbled him. Max described Diane's background as something that kept her from becoming anonymous in his classroom, as someone who was interesting and had different insight from other students. For Kevin, she stood out because of the "incredible journey" she'd been on before stepping into his class. Kevin also saw Diane's work in his class as possibly benefiting from her experiences, though not centered upon the past.

Looking over those comments that I found reminded me of how dazzled I was by the work that she was doing. It did seem like she was really bringing maximum effort to every assignment. In one I noted that she had—it was already a technically demanding assignment . . . she had made it even more technically [demanding] than it already was, so she was not trying to do the path of least resistance at any time.

It seems like she built in her poems with some potentially sensitive or difficult to confront autobiographical subject matter, but very fearlessly and . . . not in a way where she expected the material to carry the poem or speak for itself or anything like that. She was interested in transforming it into art not just in talking about herself . . . although she has had this really eventful, really interesting life, I didn't always feel like the poems she was writing were autobiographical poems. I felt like there was a lot of imagination going into her work too and a lot of imaginative sympathy. It wasn't just a desire to versify journal entries or things like that.

While Kevin saw Diane as a talented writer and a grateful student, he didn't necessarily connect these two narratives. Her talent stood alone. She approached her writing "fearlessly" and with "imagination." Kevin never implied that Diane's writing was a sort of therapy for her and he made a point to say that she didn't write what seemed to be autobiographical poems. Her identity as a justice-involved person provided her with a rich pool of experience from which to draw, but the talent she showed came from her hard work and imagination.

DISCUSSION OF PROFESSORS' OVERLAPPING NARRATIVES

These professors all narrated clear memories of Diane. Max and Kevin described how learning about her incarceration actually made her stand out from the other students in their minds. It helped to set her apart from the other students. These professors all met with Diane independently and spoke with her outside of class time. They were able to see her as not just another face in the classroom, but they came to know more about her personally, about her husband, children, volunteer work, and for Keven and Max, they knew about her incarceration. This contrasts with Diane's description of her advising experience in which she narrates the advisor as making errors and not caring much about Diane's future. It also contrasts with the way Diane storied her discussion with the chair of the human services department when she first came to the university and had wanted to become an addictions counselor. Diane's narrative portrayed the chair as someone who only understood a partiality of Diane's identity, and made untrue assumptions based upon those faulty understandings.

Definite themes appear across Diane's and her professors' narratives about her experiences as a student at Eastwood University. First of all, each faculty member's narrative described Diane's past experiences as beneficial to her role as a student. None of these professors saw her role as an older, nontraditional student as something that placed her at a disadvantage. In fact, they all echoed Diane's self-perception. Her nontraditional status gave her "experience" that allowed her to bring more to the classwork.

Justine, Max, and Kevin also framed the challenges of Diane's past as a benefit to her studies. While Justine was not aware of Diane's incarceration, she said she was aware that Diane had struggled in her past, and that the knowledge of her incarceration was not surprising. Max said he saw her incarceration as interesting and something that allowed her to see the theories they were studying in more profound ways. Finally, Kevin shared that he saw Diane as grateful and this gratitude pushed her to be one of the best students he's worked with. He saw her incarceration history as something that made her a stronger student because of how she viewed her place in the classroom within the context of her past. Halkovic and Greene (2015) contend that university faculty and staff should see formerly incarcerated women through the lens of the "gifts" they bring to campus which provide great benefit to the classroom and campus community. Justine, Max, and Kevin all saw Diane's past as one that benefited the institution and the other students in their classes. They did not see her past as one that defined Diane as damaged, unprepared, or lacking in any way. While Justine and Max described Diane as not performing in the ways they would expect from the traditional successful student, they also stated that the late or incomplete assignments did not at all reflect upon her abilities as a student, nor did they portray her learning experience.

Clearly Diane was able to sense the attitudes that these professors had regarding her past, and because of this, she felt welcomed and supported. Each of Diane's professors described working with Diane outside of class, whether during advising sessions or conferences, or tutoring sessions. The narratives of Diane's learning included her making time and taking the initiative to work with faculty in more focused ways. She was able to advocate for herself and created instances in which she was able to take her learning deeper by demanding more personalized learning experiences.

All the professors narrated Diane as an active and effective participant in class discussions, so she connected not only with her professors, but also her peers. Certainly much of this came from Diane's determination to complete her degree and also her narrative of herself as a nontraditional who had something to share with her classmates. However, these three professors obviously provided classroom contexts that allowed Diane to feel she could be authentically herself. She felt safe to participate actively. She never identified herself as an outsider or stigmatized, nor did her professors narrate her in this way.

In contrast, Diane narrated the chair of the human services department as focusing upon her identity of an addict as a possible detriment. Diane's narrative identified her as surpassing her past addictions and becoming fully recovered. This was different from the chair's narrative of addiction. Diane also narrated the relationship with her first advisor as one in which she had very little personal interaction. This first advisor may have failed to serve Diane well or make any connection with her. Diane did not describe this advisor in any detail that would show that she had a relationship with him or her. The relationships that seemed to benefit Diane were true constructive sponsorships in which the sponsors provided access, opportunities, and support as Diane moved through her college experience. These three sponsors saw Diane's past as something positive, and therefore they saw her as a student with potential and promise. Justine saw Diane's past as something neutral—that it did not really affect her current identity as a student. Max saw the incarceration as something that made Diane more interesting and able to interact with the theoretical material of his course in a more complex way. Kevin saw Diane's past as something that made her grateful and made her come to college with a special appreciation that some students may have lacked. Though these three narratives of Diane's past incarceration were different, none of them narrated Diane's identity negatively because of her past. If her past affected her learning at all, it did so in intellectually and emotionally positive ways by providing her with special insight and motivation. None of these professors mentioned any stigma attached to Diane's past, nor did they indicate their knowledge of any students or others in the department stigmatizing her in any way. They likely related this to her in many small ways and through their sponsorship she was able to complete her degree successfully.

Chapter Ten

Seeing through the Sentences and into the Stories

As more incarcerated women are released and integrate back into the social fabric, Diane's narratives provide a descriptive understanding of what a prison to school pipeline might involve with the best conditions provided. The perceptions of her professors can also instruct us as can the ways university faculty and staff supported or contradicted Diane's narratives of her identities. Diane narrated her identity as a student, and simultaneously provided a counternarrative to the accepted stories of traditional college students. While she was white, financially stable, and had some experience with college in the past, she wasn't eighteen years old and straight from high school. Instead, she was older and formerly incarcerated. She had several children, one of whom was a traditional college student. Still, Diane was able to narrate her place in higher education based upon her identity as a learner, which stayed firm throughout her incarceration. She also had a model from her younger days, a woman whom she had admired when she was a college student before her incarceration.

While Diane's original plan was to attend college to become an addictions counselor, she found that the disciplinary understanding of addict did not complement her own personal narrative of addiction, and she rejected that path. Instead, Diane found that the English professors reinforced her counternarrative, describing her strengths as a student originating from her nontraditional status. Those professors who knew of her past incarceration, Max and Kevin, saw the incarceration itself as an experience beneficial to her education. This past was not a detriment or a weakness or a stigma of criminal behavior or victimhood, but rather it was something that "made her interesting" and that inspired gratitude and deeper insights into the texts they

115

read and wrote in class. The narrative of addiction was never even mentioned within the context of her learning in this discipline.

Diane felt she fit into the English department because there were faculty who took special interest in her, and because her personal narrative identities were reinforced. Faculty remembered her, and said she was one of their best students. Unfortunately, Diane's professors did not express an understanding that her last semester was a struggle. Neither were they aware of the challenges with her previous advisor. Professors all expressed sensing that Diane was grateful for her experiences as a student. For Kevin, Diane's gratitude was central to his memories of her. Diane, throughout all her interviews only described gratitude twice. Once she mentioned she was grateful for the support of her professors and classmates:

> I think that's what kept me coming back, was just that feeling of family and support and encouragement. I didn't wanna let people down here as much as I didn't wanna let myself down. That's the truth because you know I'm friends with a lot of people here still and people that were in my classes. Particularly older people are terrific friends and it just was the right thing at the right time and I'm so grateful for it.

She also described being grateful that she was able to be a part of this research project. She was grateful that she was asked to tell her story. However, she never described being grateful for the opportunity to attend college.

Professors, administrators, and staff must be willing to adapt as they learn to constructively sponsor formerly incarcerated women. "In order to obtain the 'gain' of literacy sponsorship . . . a university must lose at least some of its traditional power but share resources with a network of partners who offer their fraught and unpredictable learning landscape as an alternative to the seemingly safe but illusory vision of standardized classroom knowledge" (Goldblatt and Jolliffe 2014, 131). We must acknowledge that the "standardized classroom knowledge" of a traditional university is specialized, politically charged, and value-laden in that it provides or withholds access to social capital, entrance into multiple, powerful discourse communities, and social autonomy. In addition to these seemingly abstract commodities, a university education provides easier access to real physical and psychological needs such as employment, food, housing, child custody, and healthcare. The "standardized classroom knowledge" is in fact, not merely the teaching of employable skills, but social capital that can provide a less menacing road to those who are already stigmatized and continually punished long after their sentences have been served.

And yet, the reciprocal nature defined by Brandt (1998) in which a sponsor gains something through the sponsorship, comes only through the transformation of the sponsor in the case of most universities. A university may mold a student's identity to fit into particular norms, as the professor of human services attempted to mold Diane's identity. Through traditional narratives of who can learn and how she should learn, a university supports and rewards typical students who behave in typical ways. Typical students are often white, middle class, recent high school graduates whose lives are uncomplicated and who self-advocate and are good at quickly learning cultural norms and following them precisely.

In some ways Diane was the typical student. She was white and had a fairly uncomplicated current life in which she was able to be a full-time student without worrying about financial stability. She was a strong self-advocate and felt empowered to speak with her professors outside of class when she needed assistance. She came to advising meetings with direction and interests to share rather than depending wholly upon her advisor's direction. In most ways, though, she was atypical, and yet her professors in the English department were able to see beyond the stigmatized narrative she freely revealed. It is through professors such as these that the university can and will be transformed to no longer be an ivory tower withholding access to our most vulnerable citizens, but a true pipeline allowing these citizens access to the riches of our nation, and the power of true citizenship.

CORRECTIONS, LITERACY, AND ACCESS

The statistics surrounding mass incarceration in the United States are undeniably bleak due in part to the silencing of the many human beings wrapped up in the prison system. Their power is taken in retribution and then continually withheld even upon release. Within this corrections system it is often difficult to find where the "correction" is occurring, or where the rehabilitation should take place. It is undeniable that the sheer number of incarcerated people released each year will have an impact on our communities. Yet, this impact is ignored, as are the individuals who are condemned to residual punishments dictated by the stigma of being justice-involved.

I endeavored through this research and the writing of this book to begin a dialogue about women, corrections, literacy, and power. Clandinin and Connelly contend that a narrative researcher's job is not to identify truths or to persuade others, but to present stories as calls for contemplation and action. They explain, "the narrative inquirer does not prescribe general applications and uses but rather creates texts that when well done offer readers a place to imagine their own uses and applications" (2000, 42). Therefore, through these stories of Grace, Lexie, Becky, and Diane, I hope to amplify voices that have been regularly and systematically silenced, so others can not only hear them, but begin to interact and dialogue with them. Though these are but four voices, they carry important and broadly unheard stories.

The construction of these women's narratives provides insight into how reading and writing are acts that connect to identity, transition, and both positive and negative visioning and reenvisioning of lived experience. These narratives identify ways women can overcome the stigma and grand narratives placed upon justice-involved individuals. While we can learn ways that literacy can allow justice-involved women to gain access and power through the telling of their own stories and moving through higher education, this research is not offered to provide specific arguments for particular policy change nor is it shared to be seen as representing some universal truths about what it means to be a woman who has a history of incarceration. Rather, these narratives and the women who have lived through and in them, are offered to allow a deeper view into four individuals' messy, complex, and sometimes inconsistent lived experiences. Experiences cannot be measured, but can be looked at closely and, like the threads of a patterned cloth, identified as smaller colors that come together to create a full design.

The women in this study portrayed their literacy experiences as being tightly intertwined with their understandings of identity. Reading and writing were not merely activities that took place in school. These women's literacy activities moved beyond the expected books, magazines, journals. Their literacy lives were rich and allowed them to actively negotiate their lived experiences. Facebook messages and good-bye letters, poetry and romance novels, all became important markers and processes to allow these women to read and write themselves into the world. The words they wrote and read weren't merely escapism or skill building; they were identity claims and the firm grasping of a piece of the world that had been taken from them.

Clearly, we squander a great deal of potential in this country as our criminal justice system continues to warehouse, silence, and erase a huge percentage of our population. The documentation of the school to prison pipeline and the disturbingly high likelihood of recidivism should be enough to convince us that we are recklessly wasting the unrealized possibilities contained within millions of lives. Educators and administrators in higher education must take notice and take up the cause of these individuals by providing pathways to degrees and training that can turn the tide not only for individuals, but also for their children and communities. While literacy does provide power and a certain cultural capital, it provides tools to tell one's own story, but not necessarily the audience to listen. We have so much more to learn from the many women who have been tangled up in our corrections system. While the first step is listening, we must be ready to also interact, to question, and understand, and take responsibility for the ways we have unconsciously been a part of a system that has in so many ways torn apart lives, families, and communities.

POSSIBILITIES FOR FUTURE RESEARCH AND IMPLICATIONS

These studies, though deep in detail and understanding of lived experiences of formerly incarcerated women, are small in scope. Though there have been many calls for more corrections and correctional education research focused upon women (Ferraro and Moe 2003; Hinshaw and Jacobi 2015; Jacobi and Stanford 2014; Mageehon 2008; Rogers et al. 2017; Willison and O'Brien 2017), the women in this study were similar in race and in literacy level. We know that a large number of incarcerated people do not have the educational level that these women had. These women were also successfully reintegrated into society, which statistics tell us is not standard. Most individuals released from the justice system become caught in a cycle of recidivism, yet these women were able to reintegrate and find success outside of prison. This study is a step in providing an understanding of the female experience of literacy practices and incarceration and reintegration. More studies are needed to fully understand the female incarceration and reintegration experiences. More studies are needed on how formerly incarcerated women negotiate their identities, especially socially acceptable identities such as those connected with motherhood and caregiving. More narrative studies that portray the lived experiences of not only the women themselves, but also their family members, especially children, could be helpful in better understanding the impact female incarceration has on larger social factors.

As more women are being released each year, it is important that more studies are done on the impact higher education has on formerly incarcerated women's lives and the most efficacious pathways that support a prison to school pipeline. We know much statistical information about education and recidivism; however, we do not have as many qualitative, and fewer narrative studies of these individuals who attempt and succeed in higher education. Diane's experience can teach us. However, Diane's case is extremely unique. She had the financial and family support that helped her succeed. She also arrived at the university with a strong identity of a student. She and her professors saw her background not as a detriment, but as a benefit to her learning. Certainly, there are many stories that are different from Diane's stories of those who are stigmatized, who must develop their identities of students as they work through courses and learn the bureaucracy of higher education. Certainly, most formerly incarcerated people come to higher education without the financial or psychological support that Diane had. Many of these, especially women, attempt higher education while negotiating other weighty responsibilities of work and parenting. Diane's narrative can tell us much, but hers is an outlier and therefore needs additional stories to supplement the true lived experiences of women who move from prison to higher education.

As we consider the smaller sponsorships, we cannot ignore the unexpected stories of the institutional sponsors. Goldblatt and Jolliffe (2014) assert that though literacy sponsors do "gain" as Brandt (1998) defines in her theory, these gains are not the expected ones in which an entity acquires more power. In fact, "Sponsors take risks, too. Indeed sponsors can be harmed, altered, or even transformed by the population and pedagogy they contract to teach" (Goldblatt and Jolliffe 2014, 131). If the expectation is for more universities to provide transitional support for justice-involved people, and if the expectation is for prisons to truly educate the incarcerated people they claim to "correct," and even if the expectation is that public schools identify and disrupt the school to prison pipeline, there must also be an expectation that each of these institutions surrender some of their power.

While the gain will be for institutions and for society, this gain will come mainly in the face of transformation of structures. As these structures are transformed, so too will the socially constructed narratives and the lives and narrative landscapes of individuals who survive by dreaming through romance novels, and watching journals set into flames. The narratives and structures will be transformed through the powerful but tiny movements from individuals who find courage to write goodbye letters to their abusers, or tentatively read Facebook messages in search of connection with their children. These acts of reading of writing will provide, if we allow them, the empowering poetry of true connection and humanity.

Bibliography

Alexander, Michelle. 2012. *The New Jim Crow: Mass Incarceration in the Age of Colorblindness*. New York: New Books.

Appleman, Deborah. 2019. *Words No Bars Can Hold: Literacy Learning in Prison*. New York: W.W. Norton.

Arditti, Joyce A. 2012. *Parental Incarceration and the Family: Psychological and Social Effects of Imprisonment on Children, Parents, and Caregivers*. New York: NYU Press.

Aronson, Joshua, Carrie B. Fried, and Catherine Good. 2002. "Reducing the Effects of Stereotype Threat on African American College Students by Shaping Theories of Intelligence." *Journal of Experimental Social Psychology* 38, no. 2: 113–125.

Bain, Ken. 2004. *What the Best College Teachers Do*. Cambridge: Harvard University Press.

Bartholomae, David. 1986. "Inventing the University." *Journal of Basic Writing* 5, no 1: 4–23.

Bender, K. 2018. "Education Opportunities in Prison Are Key to Reducing Crime." Center for American Progress. https://www.americanprogress.org/issues/education-k-12/news/2018/03/02/447321/education-opportunities-prison-key-reducing-crime.

Berry, Patrick W. 2018. *Doing Time, Writing Lives: Refiguring Literacy and Higher Education in Prison*. Carbondale: Southern Illinois University Press.

Bir, Beth, and Mondrail Myrick. 2015. "Summer Bridge's Effects on College Student Success." *Journal of Developmental Education*: 22–30.

Branch, Kirk. 2009. "What No Literacy Means: Literacy Events in the Absence of Literacy." *Reflections* 9, no. 3: 52.

Brandt, Deborah. 1998. "Sponsors of Literacy." *College Composition and Communication* 49, no. 2: 165–185.

Brandt, Deborah, and K. Clinton. 2002. "Limits of the Local: Expanding Perspectives on Literacy as Social Practice." *Journal of Literacy Research* 34, no. 3: 337–356.

Britz, Johannes J. 2004. "To Know or Not to Know: A Moral Reflection on Information Poverty." *Journal of Information Science* 30, no. 3: 192–204.

Brown, Marilyn, and Barbara E. Bloom. 2018. "Women's Desistance from Crime: A Review of Theory and the Role Higher Education Can Play." *Sociology Compass*: 1–11.

Burgstahler, S. E., and R. C. Cory, eds. 2010. *Universal Design in Higher Education: From Principles to Practice*. Cambridge: Harvard Education Press.

Cabrera, Nolan L., Danielle D. Miner, and Jeffrey F. Milem. 2013 "Can a Summer Bridge Program Impact First-Year Persistence and Performance?: A Case Study of the New Start Summer Program." *Research in Higher Education* 54, no. 5: 481–498.

Center, Pew. 2011. "State of Recidivism: The Revolving Door of America's Prisons." Washington, DC: Pew Charitable Trusts.

Clandinin, D. Jean, and F. Michael Connelly. 2000. *Narrative Inquiry: Experience and Story in Qualitative Research*. San Francisco: Jossey-Bass Publishers.

Clandinin, D. J., F. M. Connelly, and E. Chan. 2002. "Three Narrative Teaching Practices—One Narrative Teaching Exercise." In *Narrative Inquiry in Practice: Advancing the Knowledge of Teaching*, edited by Nona Lyons and Vicki Kubler LaBoskey, 133–145. New York: Teachers College Press.

Clandinin, D. Jean, Pam Steeves, and Vera Caine, eds. 2013. *Composing Lives in Transition: A Narrative Inquiry into the Experiences of Early School Leavers*. Emerald Group Publishing.

Connelly, F. M., and D. J. Clandinin. 1990. "Stories of Experience and Narrative Inquiry." *Educational Researcher* 19, no. 5: 2–14.

Cobbina, Jennifer E., and Kimberly A. Bender. 2012 "Predicting the Future: Incarcerated Women's Views of Reentry Success." *Journal of Offender Rehabilitation* 51, no. 5: 275–294.

Colvin, Sarah. 2015. "Why Should Criminology Care About Literary Fiction? Literature, Life Narratives and Telling Untellable Stories." *Punishment & Society* 17, no. 2: 211–229.

Craig, Cheryl J. 2007 "Story Constellations: A Narrative Approach to Contextualizing Teachers' Knowledge of School Reform." *Teaching and Teacher Education* 23, no. 2: 173–188.

Creswell, John. 2006 *Qualitative Inquiry and Research Design: Choosing among Five Approaches*.Thousand Oaks, CA: Sage Publications.

Curry, Michelle, and Tobi Jacobi. 2017. "'Just Sitting in a Cell, You and Me': Sponsoring Writing in a County Jail." *Community Literacy Journal* 12, no. 1: 5–22.

Custer, Bradley D. 2016 "College Admissions Policies for Ex-Offender Students: A Literature review." *The Journal of Correctional Education* 67, no. 2: 35–43.

Davis, Lois M., Robert Bozick, Jennifer L. Steele, Jessica Saunders, and Jeremy N. V. Miles. 2013. *Evaluating the Effectiveness of Correctional Education: A Meta-Analysis of Programs That Provide Education to Incarcerated Adults*. Rand Corporation.

Denzin, Norman K., and Yvonna S. Lincoln, eds. 2005. *The Sage Handbook of Qualitative Research* (3rd ed.).Thousand Oaks, CA: Sage Publications.

Deruy, Emily 2016. "From Convict to College Student." *The Atlantic*, August 2, 2016. Accessed October 11, 2019. https://www.theatlantic.com/education/archive/2016/08/from-convict-to-college-student/497579/.

Dewey, John. 1997. *How We Think*. New York: Courier Corporation.

Djikic, Maja, and Keith Oatley. 2014. "The Art in Fiction: From Indirect Communication to Changes of the Self." *Psychology of Aesthetics, Creativity, and the Arts* 8, no. 4: 498.

Djikic, Maja, Keith Oatley, Sara Zoeterman, and Jordan B. Peterson. 2009. "On Being Moved by Art: How Reading Fiction Transforms the Self." *Creativity Research Journal* 21 no. 1: 24–29.

Drabinski, Emily, and Debbie Rabina. 2015. "Reference Services to Incarcerated People, Part I: Themes Emerging from Answering Reference Questions from Prisons and Jails." *Reference & User Services Quarterly* 55, no. 1: 42–48.

Ellis, Carolyn, and Leigh Berger. 2003. "Their Story/My Story/Our Story: Including the Researcher's Experience in Interview Research." In *Postmodern Interviewing*, edited by Jaber F. Gubrium and James A. Holstein, 157–183. Thousand Oaks, CA: Sage Publications.

Erbe, Kimberly. 2019. "A Nice Outfit." In *Critical Perspectives on Teaching in Prison: Students and Instructors on Pedagogy Behind the Wall*, edited by Rebecca Ginsburg, 60–67. New York: Routledge.

Estrada, Felipe, and Anders Nilsson. 2012. "Does It Cost More to be a Female Offender? A Life-Course Study of Childhood Circumstances, Crime, Drug Abuse, and Living Conditions." *Feminist Criminology* 7, no. 3: 196–219.

Ferarro, Kathleen J., and Angela M. Moe. 2003. "Mothering, Crime, and Incarceration." *Journal of Contemporary Ethnography* 32, no. 1: 9–40.

Freire, Paulo. 2000. *Pedagogy of the Oppressed*. New York: Bloomsbury.

Freire, Paulo, and Donaldo Macedo. 1987. *Literacy: Reading the Word and the World*. Massachusetts: Bergin & Garvey.

Gee, James Paul. 2000. "Chapter 3: Identity as an Analytic Lens for Research in Education." *Review of Research in Education* 25, no. 1: 99–125.

———. 2014. *An Introduction to Discourse Analysis: Theory and Method.* New York: Routledge.

———. 2015. *Literacy and Education.* New York: Routledge.

Gergen, Mary M., and Kenneth J. Gergen. 2006. "Narratives in Action." *Narrative Inquiry* 16, no. 1: 112–121.

Gilardi, Silvia, and Chiara Guglielmetti. 2011 "University Life of Non-Traditional Students: Engagement Styles and Impact on Attrition." *The Journal of Higher Education* 82, no. 1: 33–53.

Ginsburg, Rebecca. 2019. *Critical Perspectives on Teaching in Prison: Students and Instructors on Pedagogy Behind the Wall.* New York: Routledge.

Goncalves, Sally Ann, and Dunja Trunk. 2014 "Obstacles to Success for the Nontraditional Student in Higher Education." *Psi Chi Journal of Psychological Research* 19, no. 4: 164–172.

Glaze, Lauren E., and Laura M. Maruschak. 2008. "Parents in Prison and Their Minor Children. US Department of Justice." *Bureau of Justice Statistics, Special Report. NCJ* 222984.

Goldblatt, Eli, and David E. Jolliffe. 2014. "The Unintended Consequences of Sponsorship." In *Literacy Economy and Power: Writing and Research after Literacy in American Lives,* edited by John Duffy, Julie Nelson Christoph, Eli Goldblatt, Rebecca S. Nelson-Nowacek, and Bryan Trabold, 127–135. Carbondale, IL: Southern Illinois University Press.

Hagan, John. 1989. "Micro- and Macro-Structures of Delinquency Causation and a Power-Control Theory of Gender and Delinquency." In *Theoretical Integration in the Study of Deviance and Crime: Problems and Prospects,* edited by Steven F. Messner, Marvin D. Krohn, and Allen E. Liska, 213–227. Albany: State University of New York Press.

Halkovic, Alexis. 2014. "Redefining Possible: Re-Visioning the Prison-to-College Pipeline." *Equity and Excellence in Education* 47, no. 4: 494–512.

Halkovic, Alexis, and Andrew Cory Greene. 2015. "Bearing Stigma, Carrying Gifts: What Colleges Can Learn from Students with Incarceration Experience." *The Urban Review* 47, no. 4: 759–782.

Heitzeg, Nancy A. 2009. "Education or Incarceration: Zero Tolerance Policies and the School to Prison Pipeline." *In Forum on Public Policy Online*, no. 2.

Hinshaw, Wendy Wolters, and Tobi Jacobi. 2015. "What Words Might Do: The Challenge of Representing Women in Prison and Their Writing." *Feminist Formations* 27, no. 1: 67–90.

hooks, bell. 2014. *Teaching to Transgress.* Routledge.

Inklebarger, Timothy. 2018. "Restricting Books behind Bars: Books-to-Prisoners Groups Face Roadblocks." *American Libraries Magazine.* https://americanlibrariesmagazine.org/2018/06/01/restricting-books-behind-bars-prison-libraries/.

Jacobi, Tobi, and Ann Folwell Stanford. 2014. *Women, Writing, and Prison: Activists, Scholars, and Writers Speak Out.* Lanham, MD: Rowman & Littlefield.

James, William. 1983. *Talks to Teachers on Psychology, and to Students on Some of Life's Ideals.* Camrbidge, MA: Harvard University Press.

Jones, Lise Ø., and Terje Manger. 2019. "Literacy Skills, Academic Self-Efficacy, and Participation in Prison Education." In *The Wiley Handbook of Adult Literacy,* edited by Dolores Perin, 151–169. Hoboken, NJ: Wiley-Blackwell.

Kahu, Ella R., and Karen Nelson. 2018. "Student Engagement in the Educational Interface: Understanding the Mechanisms of Student Success." *Higher Education Research & Development* 37, no. 1: 58–71.

Lefebvre, Henri, and Donald Nicholson-Smith. 1991. *The Production of Space.* Vol. 142. Blackwell: Oxford.

Lincoln Yvonna S., and Egon G. Guba. 1985. *Naturalistic Inquiry.* Newbury Park, CA: Sage Publications.

Lochner, Lance, and Enrico Moretti. 2004. "The Effect of Education on Crime: Evidence from Prison Inmates, Arrests, and Self-Reports." *American Economic Review* 94, no. 1: 155–189.

Lockard, Joe, and Sherry Rankins-Robertson, eds. 2018. *Prison Pedagogies: Learning and Teaching with Imprisoned Writers.* Syracuse University Press.

Mageehon, Alexandria. 2008. "Caught Up in the System: How Women Who Have Been Incarcerated Negotiate Power." *The Prison Journal* 88, no. 4: 473–492.

Maher, J. 2004. "My Way Out of This Life Is an Education." *Women's Studies Quarterly* 1, no. 2: 100–114.

McCarthy, Lucille. 1987. "Parkinson Stranger in Strange Lands." *Research in the Teaching of English* 21, no. 3: 233–265.

McQuaide, Stacy Bell. 2019. "'Go Hard': Bringing Privilege-Industry Pedagogies into a College Writing Classroom in Prison." In *Critical Perspectives on Teaching in Prison: Students and Instructors on Pedagogy Behind the Wall*, edited by Rebecca Ginsburg, 102–111. New York: Routledge.

McTier, Terrence S., Stephen Santa-Ramirez, and Keon M. McGuire. 2017. "A Prison to School Pipeline." *Journal of Underrepresented & Minority Progress* 1, no. 1: 8–22.

Mezirow, Jack. 1990. "How Critical Reflection Triggers Transformative Learning." *Fostering Critical Reflection in Adulthood* 1, no. 20: 1–6.

Mishler, Elliot G. 1991. *Research Interviewing: Context and Narrative*. Harvard University Press.

Murray, Donald. 1991 "All Writing Is Autobiography" *Composition and Communication* 42, no. 1 (Feb.): 66–74.

Muth, Bill, Elizabeth Sturtevant, and Gina Pannozzo. 2017. "Performance and Beliefs: Two Assessments of Literacy Learners in Prison Part I." *Journal of Correctional Education (1974–)* 68, no. 1: 71–96.

New London Group. 1996. "A Pedagogy of Multiliteracies: Designing Social Futures." *Harvard Educational Review* 66, no. 1: 60–92.

Novek, Eleanor. 2017. "Jail Pedagogies: Teaching and Trust in a Maximum Security Men's Prison." *Dialogues in Social Justice* 2, no. 2: 31–51.

———. 2019. "Making Meaning: Reflections on the Act of Teaching in Prison." *Review of Communication* 19, no. 1: 55–68.

Nussbaum, Martha C. 1998. *Cultivating Humanity*. Cambridge, MA: Harvard University Press.

Olesen, Virginia. 1994. "Feminisms and Models of Qualitative Research." In *Handbook of Qualitative Research*, edited by N. K. Denzin and Y. S. Lincoln, 158–174. Thousand Oaks, CA: Sage Publications.

Opsal, Tara D. 2011. "Women Disrupting a Marginalized Identity: Subverting the Parolee Identity through Narrative." *Journal of Contemporary Ethnography* 40, no. 2: 135–167.

Panacci, Adam G. 2015. "Adult Students in Higher Education: Classroom Experiences and Needs." *College Quarterly* 18, no. 3.

Patterson, Margaret. 2018. "Incarcerated Adults with Low Skills: Findings from the 2014 PIAAC Prison Study." *Essential Education* 8, no. 1: 14–24.

Polkinghorne, Donald. 1988. *Narrative Knowing and the Human Sciences*. Albany: SUNY Press.

Reiter, Keramet. 2014. "Making Windows in Walls: Strategies for Prison Research." *Qualitative Inquiry* 20, no. 4: 417–428.

———. 2017. *Mass Incarceration*. Oxford, UK: Oxford University Press.

Rogers, Laura, Wendy Hinshaw, Corey Holding, and Tobi Jacobi. 2017. "Bending Bars: A Dialogue between Four Prison Teacher-Researchers." *Survive and Thrive: A Journal for Medical Humanities and Narrative as Medicine* 3, no. 1, article 14.

Sampson, Robert J., and John H. Laub. 1995. *Crime in the Making: Pathways and Turning Points Through Life*. Cambridge, MA: Harvard University Press.

Sawyer, Wendy, and Peter Wagner. 2019. "Mass Incarceration: The Whole Pie 2019." *Prison Policy Initiative*. https://www.prisonpolicy.org/reports/pie2019.html.

Schaafsma, David, and Ruth Vinz. 2011. *On Narrative Inquiry: Approaches to Language and Literacy (An NCRLL Volume). Language & Literacy Series. NCRLL Series*. New York: Teachers College Press.

Shapiro, Dough, Afet Dundar, Faye Huie, Phoebe Khasiala Wakhungu, Xin Yuan, Angel Nathan, and Ayesha Bhimdiwali. 2017. "Completing College: A National View of Student Completion Rates–Fall 2011 Cohort."

Silver, Patricia, Andrew Bourke, and K. C. Strehorn. 1998. "Universal Instructional Design in Higher Education: An Approach for Inclusion." *Equity & Excellence* 31, no. 2: 47–51.

Smarsh, Sarah. 2017. "Poor Teeth." *Aeon*, 22 March. Accessed December 13, 2019. aeon.co/essays/there-is-noshame-worse-than-poor-teeth-in-a-rich-world.

Smith, Dorothy. 1987. *The Everyday World as Problematic: A Sociology for Women*. Boston: Northeastern University Press.

Smith, Linda Tuhiwai. 2013. *Decolonizing Methodologies: Research and Indigenous Peoples*. Zed Books Ltd.

Sokoloff, Natalie J., and Anika Schenck-Fontaine. 2017. "College Programs in Prison and upon Reentry for Men and Women: A Literature Review." *Contemporary Justice Review* 20, no. 1: 95–114.

Soria, Krista M., and Michael J. Stebleton. 2012. "First-Generation Students' Academic Engagement and Retention." *Teaching in Higher Education* 17, no. 6: 673–685.

Speer, Nicole K., Jeremy R. Reynolds, Khena M. Swallow, and Jeffrey M. Zacks. 2009. "Reading Stories Activates Neural Representations of Visual and Motor Experiences." *Psychological Science* 20, no. 8: 989–999.

St. John, Victor J., and Kwan-Lamar Blount-Hill. 2019. "Place, Space, Race, and Life during and after Incarceration: Dismantling Mass Incarceration through Spatial and Placial Justice." *Harvard Journal of African American Public Policy*: 46–54.

Sue, Derald Wing, Christina M. Capodilupo, Gina C. Torino, Jennifer M. Bucceri, Aisha Holder, Kevin L. Nadal, and Marta Esquilin. 2007. "Racial Microaggressions in Everyday Life: Implications for Clinical Practice." *American Psychologist* 62, no. 4: 271.

Swecker, Hadyn K., Mathew Fifolt, and Linda Searby. 2013. "Academic Advising and First-Generation College Students: A Quantitative Study on Student Retention." *NACADA Journal* 33, no. 1: 46–53.

Sweeney, Megan. 2010. *Reading Is My Window: Books and the Art of Reading in Women's Prisons*. Chapel Hill, NC: The University of North Carolina Press.

Thompson, Melissa, and Milena Petrovic. 2009. "Gendered Transitions: Within-Person Changes in Employment, Family, and Illicit Drug Use." *Journal of Research in Crime and Delinquency* 46, no. 3: 377–408.

US Department of Education. 2016. "State and Local Expenditures on Corrections and Education." A brief from the U.S. Department of Education, Policy and Program Studies Service. https://www2.ed.gov/rschstat/eval/other/expenditures-corrections-education/brief.pdf.

Vacca, James S. 2004. "Educated Prisoners Are Less Likely to Return to Prison." *Journal of Correctional Education* 55, no. 4: 297–305.

Visher, Christy A., and Jeremy Travis. 2003 "Transitions from Prison to Community: Understanding Individual Pathways." *Annual Review of Sociology*, no. 29: 89–113.

Wald, Johanna, and Daniel J. Losen. 2003. "Defining and Redirecting a School-to-Prison Pipeline." *New Directions for Youth Development*, no. 99: 9–15.

Walmsley, Roy. 2016. "World Prison Brief." Institute for Criminal Policy Research database.

Weimer, Maryellen. 2002. *Learner-Centered Teaching: Five Key Changes to Practice*. Hoboken, NJ: John Wiley & Sons.

Wesely, Jennifer K. 2018. "Co-Constituting Narrative: The Role of Researcher Identity Bids in Qualitative Interviews with Women Ex-Offenders." *Criminal Justice Studies* 31, no. 3: 213–229.

Willison, Judith S., and Patricia O'Brien. 2017. "A Feminist Call for Transforming the Criminal Justice System." *Affilia* 32, no. 1: 37–49.

Wiltse, Ed. 2011. "Doing Time in College: Student-Prisoner Reading Groups and the Object(s) of Literary Study." *Critical Survey* 23, no. 3: 6–22.

Woodiwiss, J., Kate Smith, and Kelly Lockwood. 2017. *Feminist Narrative Research*. London: Palgrave Macmillan.

Wright, Emily M., Dana D. DeHart, Barbara A. Koons-Witt, and Courtney A. Crittenden. 2013. "'Buffers' against Crime? Exploring the Roles and Limitations of Positive Relationships Among Women in Prison." *Punishment & Society* 15, no. 1: 71–95.

Index

About the Author

Melanie N. Burdick, PhD, is a professor of English and director of the Center for Teaching Excellence and Learning at Washburn University in Topeka, Kansas. She is the coauthor with Heidi Hallman of the book *Community Fieldwork in Teacher Education: Theory and Practice*. She has authored or coauthored a number of articles and book chapters in the areas of writing pedagogy, community-engaged learning, and faculty development. She has co-taught a creative writing class in the medium/maximum security women's prison at the Topeka Correctional Facility and serves on the editorial board of the *Journal of Correctional Education*.

www.ingramcontent.com/pod-product-compliance
Lightning Source LLC
Chambersburg PA
CBHW022324280326
41932CB00010B/1214